SELL TO THE RICH

The Insider's Handbook to Selling Luxury

Jeffrey Shaw

Printed in the United States of America
10 9 8 7 6 5 4 3 2 1

ISBN: 978-0-9995187-1-7 (paperback)
ISBN: 978-0-9995187-2-4 (e-book)

Edited by Kristina Paider
Cover Design by Sharon Hobson
Book Design by Choi Messer

ABOUT THE AUTHOR

FROM HUMBLE BEGINNINGS, JEFFREY SHAW became one of the most preeminent portrait photographers in the United States. His portraits have appeared on *The Oprah Winfrey Show* and *CBS News*, in *People* and *O Magazine*, and hang in the halls of Harvard University.

Today, Jeffrey speaks about luxury buyer behavior and how to sell to an affluent clientele at events and conferences for organizations such as ASID, NKBA, The Pearl Collective, Design Trust, and Luxury Home Design Summit, and for corporations like Verizon and BMW. He is the author of *LINGO (2018)*, *The Self-Employed Life (2021)*, and *Sell to the Rich* (2025), a LinkedIn Learning Instructor, and host of *The Self-Employed Life* podcast.

Jeffrey is also the founder of The Exceptional Business Academy and The Self-Employed Business Institute. His TEDx Talk, "The Validation Paradox: Finding Your Best Through Others" is featured on TED.com, and he is responsible for the creation of National Self-Employed Day, which falls on May 4th of the U.S. National Calendar and honors the hard work and contribution of independent business owners.

His obsessions are many including chai, macarons, gardening, and Barbra Streisand. While clearly he cares a great deal about his work, he's pretty convinced he'll be remembered most for hosting Waffle Sundays at his home and that suits him just fine.

*Dedicated to forty years of photography clients who
invited me into their homes, welcomed me into their families,
and inspired me to find more in myself than I ever imagined.*

CONTENTS

ELEMENT III: LUXURY BUYER BEHAVIOR

ELEMENT IV: LUXURY BRANDING

Contents

WHO YOU'RE
MEANT TO SERVE

Luxury isn't a market category or a price point. It's a chosen way to see and appreciate the world.

WHO YOU'RE MEANT TO SERVE

LUXURY IS MUCH MORE THAN a market category, a price point, or a logo on a product. It's a way of being. It's how you choose to see the world, the beauty that encompasses you, the value that is appreciated, and what you offer in return. It's a standard you choose to live by or a standard you strive to achieve.

Luxury is a perspective that shapes the experiences, relationships, and values perceived on both sides of the equation. It's truly a give and receive. The exceptional experience you create for others brings out the best in you and fulfills your aspirations, and luxury becomes synonymous with gratitude. It's the artistry in the details, the mood of the environments, the elegance in restraint, and the strength in a quiet confidence that speaks to the heart of those who choose to live, purchase, and deliver with intention in the spirit of luxury.

This book is for small business owners currently serving the luxury market who want to refine their business, serve their clients even better, and elevate their business—as well as for emerging leaders looking to step into the luxury world and carve their own path toward serving high-end clients. This book can serve as a how-to handbook for sales associates and leaders of large luxury brands who are driving the market forward. Whether you are in the early stages of business or career or decades in, serving the luxury market is a never-ending growth opportunity. Sharing my forty-plus years of experience in the luxury space, I'm confident there will be value here for you.

This book is about nurturing a state of mind and a way of being that is necessary to serve this often-misunderstood clientele. It's about understanding the seemingly complex behavior and psychology of the luxury buyer and implementing unique strategies fitting the expectations and standards of a *deserving*, not just discerning, client base.

There's also an even bigger dream here. One that stretches beyond luxury brands. Imagine a world where every business adopted just a touch of the principles traditionally reserved for luxury brands. Imagine everyday businesses standing out because they've mastered the art of delivering beyond expectation, with grace, consistency, and refinement. Imagine customers everywhere experiencing service that makes them feel valued and understood—and imagine the ripple effect that level of quality and care could have on our world. It's not just about selling products and offering services. It's about cultivating a world where exceptional is the standard and connection is revered.

This is the art and aspiration of luxury and this book is your invitation to bring that aspiration to fruition.

I'll be honest. I could never have written this book at any other time in my life. It's taken a tremendous amount of inner work to unpack the journey and be able to communicate the heart and sincere feelings that are necessary to truly succeed in the luxury market space. While I was conscious of my strategies and could have taught those in the past, I'm afraid my thoughts may have come across as too crass if I tried to write this book sooner. Let's face it—*Sell to the Rich* is a pretty blunt title and I was immediately challenged by some to "soften" it. Perhaps *Sell to the Affluent*, or *How to Sell to the Luxury Market*. I get it, I truly do. But I stuck with *Sell to the Rich* for the double-entendre that is encapsulated here.

It's not simply about selling to rich people. I want you to see and value the richness in yourself. I want you to connect with others who hold the same values, represent a richness in life, and sell that. It's not about luxury in one dimension—it's about fully dimensional luxury, in all its aspects. It's about discovering in yourself an honest desire to be the best, most abundant and passionate version of yourself that you could ever imagine. It's about finding more in yourself than you ever thought possible. It's about wanting to do better, be better, embrace growth, and raise standards for yourself, those around you, and quite possibly, the whole world. It's a desire to be exceptional in a world where even being great isn't good enough anymore. It's about having a bigger, richer vision for yourself and the world you live in.

That's why this is more than a business book. It's more than a how-to-succeed book. It's about more than selling to affluent buyers, but rather, about committing to all of the richness available in life—for you, others, and the world. It's about creating the most beautiful of environments, paying attention to the most minute details, offering the finest quality, and building the strongest bonds. It's about seeing everything at an entirely different level: the luxury level.

In coaching luxury brands and small business owners, I often help them see the difference by comparing the ordinary world and the exceptional world. The ordinary world is where most of life exists. It's mainstream and meets minimum standards. It's where great is the goal. Where great quality and great customer service exist but no longer stand out because customers expect great. In the ordinary world, businesses focus on branding when in reality, in order to appeal to the luxury buyer, you need to create emotional resonance. A much taller order. In the ordinary world, the message that business is all about relationships is drilled in when really it should be about how to build unbreakable bonds because the relationship is that strong. In the ordinary world, businesses focus on great customer service and in the exceptional world, the focus is on a life-transforming experience. Where others might work on their mindset, motivation, and a "fake it until you make it" attitude, to truly be exceptional and deserving of the success you seek, you learn you have to retrain your own way of thinking and embody the life of those you are meant to serve.

The goal is to reach the clientele that you are meant to serve and receive all that is meant for you. It's a reciprocal arrangement. That's why this is more than a business book.

It's your call to greatness: your call to see, acknowledge, appreciate, and own your worth.

The beautiful thing is—in your call to greatness and on the journey of building a luxury brand or serving a discerning clientele—you are not alone. I believe it's true that often people see more in us than we see in ourselves, which is the theme of my TEDx talk, The Validation Paradox. I also think it's even more true in the luxury market. The luxury client likes to be the one to discover something new, find the perfect service provider, and then share with all their friends. They highly respect effort, cleverness, and smart business. They value integrity and authenticity. If they sense you are taking action with good intentions, operating in integrity, and are trustworthy, they will gladly support you in your endeavors.

And a journey it is. I'm speaking to you now from the vantage point of a forty-plus year career as a portrait photographer for affluent families. I have popped champagne, went on vacations to envy, and worked with a client list to die for. But that is far from where I started.

◆

I TOOK A DEEP BREATH as I tapped on the square metal numbers on the black pay phone, calling into my voicemail. Each key had a corresponding harmonic tone—bleep bleep bloop beep bop—you might remember when you had to call a phone number and put in a code to retrieve voicemail messages. I stood outside the front entrance to the local general store's entrance—a faded brown screen door that slapped me in the back every time it flung open, and made a loud thud every time it banged shut—about six times a minute, thanks to hordes of kids running in and out, excited about their purchase of Skittles, Nerds, and Pop Rocks.

My thoughts drifted off with the summer clouds, contemplating the possibilities of my future: leaving my struggling photography business and small-town life behind and launching an upscale portrait photography business in one of the most affluent zip codes in the U.S.

Standing where I was at this moment, in my bathing suit, t-shirt, and flip flops—becoming the premier family portrait photographer in Connecticut, maybe even in the U.S., seemed as ridiculous as it did impossible. I was in a state park campground in the Adirondacks, where my parents, siblings, aunts, uncles, cousins, and grandparents, had pulled alongside campers and boats and pitched tents for the same vacation we'd taken to the same place for all of my 23 years of life. I wasn't ungrateful. But this just wasn't a fit for me. Nothing about it fit me. My small country hometown wasn't a fit. My clothes weren't a fit, and for sure, my photography business in its current state wasn't a fit. In fact, it was failing.

By all metrics of measurement, my dream was irrational at best and crazy at worst. On top of that, people made me anxious. I had no real business experience. I was extremely introverted. And I knew nothing about rich people.

But I did know one thing. And I felt it with deep conviction: I knew who I was meant to serve.

In the three years since graduating photography school and opening my business in my hometown about two hours north of New York City, I learned what it felt like to be completely misaligned with the people I was trying to serve. The frustration of day after day trying to convince people of the value of what you believe in with all your might when they simply don't get it. Or aren't willing to pay for it.

Having to take on work that feels degrading but you think you're supposed to start from the ground up when you're building a business or advancing your career. Just grinning and bearing it because there are bills to pay.

Fighting an uphill battle to build a business just didn't feel right to me. Feeling out of sync with the people around me made me realize an important lesson, though. There's got to be some audience of people out there that think like I do, have similar values, and are willing to pay for what I have to offer. And to me, the idea of preserving precious family memories felt like nothing could be more valuable. But I guess when you're barely getting by day-by-day—which was the case in my hometown—who can think that far ahead?

I knew that my camera was my way out of what felt like limited options and out of feeling insignificant. I knew that this business wasn't going to cut it in this working-class town. I was at a cross-roads. I knew that I had to make a choice, and soon. Either I had to continue offering low-cost senior portraits, doing catalogs, or shooting weddings (which made me so nervous I lost sleep the whole week before) and working three or four times harder to pay my bills, or I needed to find people who valued what I offered. And I believed those people were in the bordering state of Connecticut, which I heard was where wealthy people lived.

Having barked up the wrong tree and feeling misaligned with the people around me for the first three years of business made it clear who I was meant to serve: people who had discretionary income. Wealthy families, who thought long-term, had the money to invest in the future, and put family first. Ideal clients who I came to identify as family-centric wealthy families. Not just anyone I could take a picture of, not even all wealthy families. But those who put family first and whose affluence afforded them all the support they needed to make their families a priority and who valued anything that would capture and preserve the near perfect lifestyle they worked so hard to create.

The clearer my vision became, the more impassioned I felt in my soul that these people were more than ideal clients. They were the people I was meant to partner with, to share my talent with—to serve. These were the people I was eager to learn more about. Willing to put aside any preconceived notions and be empathetic and open—in mind and heart—to what I didn't know.

I had recently donated a gift certificate for my services to a silent auction at a gala fundraiser for The Junior League of Greenwich. I didn't even know what a silent auction was until a chance conversation with a dentist filled me in.

Once explained, it made immediate sense for me to donate a photography package. I got to display a large wall portrait on an easel at the event. Display space was limited, so I advocated for myself to show a portrait large enough to be representative of my work (and impress people). From what I knew about the gala and the location, the attendees would be my ideal high-end clients who I believed would see the value in my style of environmental portrait photography—the one thing I loved to do. I even considered attending the Phantom of the Opera-themed event, and I negotiated for a free ticket. However, I didn't go—I was way too intimidated.

My theory was that if someone bought my portrait package donation, it'd be a massive opportunity—a doorway into the market. I believed that one gig would be enough to create the bridge to get me from where I was standing at this campground to where I wanted to be: serving an affluent client base who valued my unparalleled, legacy photography. I just needed proof that I was headed in the right direction and today could be the day. I was so hopeful that someone would bid on my silent auction donation or see my work on display, and open that door in Connecticut. One chance was all I needed.

One nod of approval. One person who said yes could launch my future. Today could be the day.

I waited anxiously to hear whether there was a message. I shifted my weight from one side to the other, sliding my fingers up and down the metal coil of the payphone, clinging to it like the lifeline that it was.

And then…

…there it was.

…I heard the words that would forever change the trajectory of my career.

"Hello, this is Barbara from Greenwich, Connecticut."

◆

EVERYTHING I IMAGINED LITERALLY DID come true after receiving that voicemail. That's not to say six figures instantly arrived in my bank account, or the phone immediately started ringing off the hook. It's also not to say it was easy, or came fast, but it was my truth as much as it was my true calling. Barbara hired me to do her daughter's portrait. She turned out to be the wife of the CEO of one the world's largest food brands and I went on to photograph their daughter annually for sixteen consecutive years.

That one client wasn't a lucky break. It was confirmation that I got it right. I identified who my ideal clients were, did the work to learn about them and their lifestyle and built a business that they could recognize as "for them." What came first, before the relationship, the assignment, the voicemail, or even the silent auction donation, was being clear on who I was meant to serve. What came first was a deep conviction within myself and my instinct for where I belonged. Those things led to the actions that set the right things into motion.

This may be the most important take-away I have for you. If you feel, in your heart, mind, and soul, that this who you are meant to serve—the luxury client—then there's much for you to gain in this book. Because you have stepped beyond working hard, beyond trying to please, beyond "serving" in an accommodating sense into truly serving because you care. That's a drive that will keep you going and practically guarantee your success. It may surprise you to learn that this knowing is incredibly important in order to sell to the rich.

I often refer to it as clean energy because this clientele that you strive to serve—the high-end, luxury, affluent, high-net-worth, ultra-high-net-worth, or whatever other name there may be—is highly perceptive. The lesson here is that many people may think that people with money tend to be shallow or surface-level, or that they are difficult, demanding, or discerning, which is more often said as an underhanded sneer than a compliment. However, in my experience, the truth is when you truly get to know what makes them tick and understand their behavior without all the labels, judgments, and stereotypes, they are the most intuitive, sophisticated, energy-reading, intention-aware people you will ever serve.

One thing I insist on as I share the most vulnerable parts of my life and the insider secrets to serving this clientele is that we do so without judgment. That our intentions are clear and clean. That we have a reason to serve this clientele that is bigger than the money, prestige, or any reason other than serving those you believe you are meant to serve. Yes, of course there is money and prestige, and, there is so much more and I wish it all for you. But if it feels to your potential clients that you prioritize money and prestige more than you do being at your best, valuing their relationship, and serving them, it will repel them. If you think the roads are paved with gold when serving the luxury market, they will sniff that out and it will not work.

Whether you are a small luxury business owner, leader of a large luxury brand, or a sales associate of a luxury brand, you can only sell to the rich and succeed in the long run if you do so coming from a place of integrity, have a strong desire to serve, and because you know yourself so well it is clear to you that this is who you are meant to serve. If they feel that "clean energy" and honest intention to serve them, they can become your most loyal customers, strongest advocates, best brand ambassadors, and most easy-to-work-with ideal customers you could ever have dreamed of. But it all begins with you.

The contrast of the moment at the pay phone was extreme. Vacationing with my family at a campground in the woods, standing outside of a general store on a pay phone, wearing a bathing suit and t-shirt, mid-twenties, and I'm receiving a call from a highly sophisticated affluent woman in Connecticut. None of it made sense—yet it all made sense. Although I suspected where I would end up in life would look nothing like where I started without any idea how that would happen, I knew for certain what I was meant to do and who I was meant to work with. I felt it in my bones and my gut that these were the families that would value what I did. I also took smart action to put myself in front of the right people in the right place at the right time. Success felt inevitable even though, at that moment at the pay phone, it couldn't have looked more unrealistic. My gut may have only suspected what the future would hold for me, but I knew with complete certainty, with every fiber of my being, who I was meant to serve. For whatever reason—because that wasn't anything familiar to me before. But I knew. It was never about money, prestige, or anything else. It was about those that would appreciate my talent and with whom I shared my value for preserving beautiful moments in life and who held similar standards for perfection and detail. In many ways, I felt more at home serving this clientele than even in my own family. And that is why I believe it worked.

I am fortunate to have had much support in multiple forms as I built my business. I have countless stories of incredibly influential and well-known public figures who bolstered my career not only by providing referrals but even sharing private country club and private school lists. Shh…don't tell anyone. Perhaps my favorite story of someone stepping up for me was when I stopped by a very upscale children's clothing boutique to introduce myself, since their customers were the customers I wanted to meet. The owner was very kind and quite interested in the sample portraits I brought along. She introduced herself as Susie Hilfiger and when I commented on the small shelf of men's clothing off to the side, she mentioned that her then-husband designed clothes, so she gave him a small shelf space. Without hesitation, Susie went on to introduce me to some of the most influential people in town—who hired me, passed my name around, got me involved in other silent auction fundraisers, and invited me to parties. Each and every one of them was generous, supportive, and so kind.

Do I think maybe I was lucky? Perhaps. Do I think this can happen for everyone and that everyone you meet is as kind? Perhaps not all. But by and large, I do believe people see more in us than we see in ourselves. The sophisticated, highly perceptive, keenly aware luxury buyer especially so. Their antennas are up. They are unfortunately used to being targeted. Their high standards and attention to detail have honed their instinct. Just like how the energy of suspicion, misdirected intention, and being salesy repels the luxury buyer, if they sense and see in you a greater potential and new discovery, you may gain the greatest advocates you can ever imagine.

Will everyone you meet be the ideal luxury customer? Of course not. But that's true in all market segments. Stereotypes and stories we often hear can lead us to believe the affluent client is more difficult than most. If you believe that, then you are already starting off on the wrong foot.

Too often in business, across all markets and socioeconomic groups, we see business owners and sales associates who have an innate attitude against their customers. Against! There's an atmosphere of friction from the beginning and again, this highly perceptive client knows it. I had a very different perspective. I loved my clients before I even met them. Every future client was like waiting for the person of my dreams to show up. As I got to know them and their families, gained a deeper understanding of their often very complicated lives, and watched them often hold it all together, this big life of theirs—while being gracious to me—was true class. I loved them before I met them and only grew to love them more.

If you are holding onto to assumptions, judgments, and stereotypes, you can't be surprised that's what you'll see in return. It's like looking into a mirror and expecting to see something different than what you place in front of it. You won't succeed that way and my goal here is for you to succeed. I can honestly say that in forty years of serving a very demanding clientele and being responsible for how they look in their photographs, came across to all their friends, and essentially holding their public image in my hands, there were just two clients that I disliked. One client I fired because she was consistently a no-show for appointments and the other, I refused to work with the moment she called. Her arrogance was other level. Two out of thousands over forty years. I'll take those odds. And I'll give myself some credit because I did the inner work to be clear and clean in my intentions and all my actions. I got the clients I deserved and so can you.

The question is this:

Who do you have to become, how do you need to come across, and what do you need to do to be deserving of the attention, support, and business of the most astute clientele on the planet?

Are you ready to step into your greatness?

Now, let's get down to how you can get the most out of this book.

First of all, please understand this. This is a practical, real-life book. The advantage of not having come from a world of luxury is that everything was interesting and new along my journey and I was insanely curious. It magnified my ability to objectively observe everything. To observe, study, test, and be curious without judgment or assumptions. So, my perspective is far more "from the trenches" than research and data driven. While I appreciate the value that data, trends, and research can offer us—and there may be more in the luxury space than anywhere else I have ever seen—it is my perspective that nothing, *NOTHING* will ever be more important than actually understanding your buyers, what they think, the emotions that drive them, their lifestyles, and their behaviors. A real-life in real-time from-the-trenches perspective also enables you to change quickly as needed. Luxury buyers are trendsetters and react to almost everything more quickly than everyone else. The first to spot a hot fashion trend and equally fast to react to changes in the economy and society. They are often the first to respond in an economic downturn and the first to recover.

By definition, research, data, and trends can only be observed in hindsight. They explain what was and can be used to predict the future. But observation, deep understanding, and what's offered in this book can be used in the moment. Adapt as you go, but I believe the way I speak about selling to the rich is long-lasting and customizable and can support you for many, many years.

Which is why this book is intended to be read in a non-linear format. It was inspired by a series of articles I wrote for my Diamond Edge newsletter, which have been expanded and re-mastered into a broader trove of luxury examples, in much more detail and a deeper level of conversation. It's written so you don't have to read it in order from cover to cover. Of course, you can and perhaps you will the first time. But then my hope is it stays nearby and serves as an ongoing resource. Have a difficult customer? There's advice for that. Confused about the behavior of a client? There's an explanation for that. Know that you are probably in your own way? There's guidance for that.

First, the book is divided into six Elements (each rare and special like a precious metal). Within each Element are individual sections covering a broad range of instances and experiences that you are likely to encounter serving the luxury buyer. Again, coming from the very personal and intimate exposure I had with the clientele.

For easy reference, diamonds on the outer edges of the pages correspond to the Element number, so you'll always know which Element you are in or want to refer to in the future.

Throughout each Element, there are numerous highlighted luxury brand stories that I call Gems. These unique and often never-heard-of-before stories are designed to inspire you and encourage you to think creatively. Luxury is not cookie-cutter. Use these stories to get your creative juices flowing and consider how you might be able to apply similar ideas and solutions to your situation regardless of how out of the box or different your industry is.

- **Element I: Luxury Philosophies**—Ways of looking at the luxury market you may never have considered before.
- **Element II: Luxury Service Mindset**—How you need to think differently as a luxury provider.
- **Element III: Luxury Buyer Behavior**—This is by far the largest section because nothing is more important than deeply understanding your buyer.
- **Element IV: Luxury Branding**—More than the obvious, it's about creating emotional resonance and alignment.
- **Element V: Luxury Customer Relationship**—Way beyond service, this is about creating bonds and brand obsession.
- **Element VI: Luxury Sales**—Deepening and understanding the moment of commitment.

It may surprise you that a book called *Sell to the Rich* has sales as the last Element. As I stated, the book is non-linear and does not have to be read in a particular order. However, there is an intended sequence here.

I have to go on a bit of a tangent to explain. When I was writing my first book, *LINGO*, my editor, brilliant confidante, and all-around great friend, AJ Harper said to me that my genius (her word, not mine) was my ability to create environments for the results I wanted. That immediately rang true for me being an on-location or environmental photographer. My style and the portraits I captured were entirely inspired first by the environment. The results I got were the result of the environments I created.

AJ pointed out that my first book, *LINGO,* was about creating an environment through brand messaging to attract ideal clients. My second book, *The Self-Employed Life,* was about the entire environment of running your own business, literally referring to it as The Self-Employed Ecosystem.

This book is yet another environment: the luxury environment. An integrated system of who you need to be, the way you need to think, the understanding you must have, and the actions you need to take in order to win the business of this uncompromising clientele. It's imbued in the quality, it's in the presentation of products in services, it's infused in the atmosphere of all interactions with the luxury buyer, it's in the culture of the business, embedded in the brand, and it comforts your customers, letting them know they are exactly where they are meant to be.

That's why the Elements are offered in the order that they are. It's why Sales is last because everything before that is necessary before you can sell to the rich effectively.

While it was clear to me for forty years that I was meant to serve affluent family-centric people as their photographer, it's equally clear to me now that I am meant to serve you, my dear reader. Whether you currently have a luxury business, aspire to build one, are a sales associate for a luxury brand, or have an everyday business that you want to take to a whole other level, this book is meant to serve you.

My intention is for this to be a how-to handbook that is readily available for you. At any given time, you may feel you need to work on one area of your business or yourself and you can turn to that Element. That's what will make this collection an ongoing resource. But please don't disregard that the whole makes up the entire environment. Each Element and each section is part of the ecosystem. Collectively, I'd like to believe it's the whole picture.

A portrait if you will, of you serving those you are meant to serve.

COTY
An Unwavering Vision

FRANÇOIS COTY WAS BORN JOSEPH Marie François Spoturno in 1874 in Ajaccio, Corsica, to a modest family. After losing his father at a young age, François' mother struggled to provide for their family.

As a young man, François studied in Marseille and later Paris, where he discovered his passion for perfumery. Under the guidance of a skilled chemist and perfumer, he became captivated by the art of creating fragrances that could evoke deep emotions and create imaginative stories. François envisioned making fine perfumes accessible to a broader audience, a revolutionary idea at the time.

In 1904, he crafted his first perfume, La Rose Jacqueminot. When the high-end department store he approached showed little interest, François staged a bold demonstration. Legend has it that he "accidentally" dropped a bottle on the floor, filling the air with its alluring aroma. Customers were immediately drawn to the scent, and the store quickly agreed to carry his line.

François understood that a perfume's allure extended beyond its fragrance. He partnered with artists like René Lalique to design elegant bottles, turning his perfumes into coveted luxury items. With bold advertising and mass distribution, he revolutionized the perfume industry, combining artistry with business savvy.

Within a decade, Coty's name became synonymous with luxury, and his empire expanded into cosmetics. Despite later personal and financial difficulties, François Coty's vision redefined the fragrance industry and his rags-to-riches story is a testament to the power of vision, resilience, and creativity.

ELEMENT I

Luxury Philosophies

For as long as there's an opportunity to see things differently, there's an opportunity for things to be different.

LUXURY PHILOSOPHIES
Introduction

IMAGINE YOU'RE HANGING A PIECE of art in your home, carefully considering its placement in the room. Or in my case, the countless wall portraits I hung at my client's homes. You approach it with care, standing close to the wall as you measure the exact spot to place the nail. With precision, you tap in the hook, ensuring it's secure and that the piece is perfectly positioned. Once you've hung it, you gently tug to confirm it's stable, maybe even nudge one side or the other until you're confident it's level. And then what? You step back.

You step back to see the artwork or a portrait in the context of the room, considering how it looks in its surroundings, perhaps even adjusting it once more for that final touch.

Stepping back like this allows us to see things in context from a different perspective. Often, we find that when we step back, we notice things we couldn't see up close, seeing how the elements connect with their broader environment. This idea of stepping back isn't just applicable to hanging artwork; it's also a powerful approach to understanding business and the world of luxury.

Most of us who work in the luxury market don't come from the same world as our clients. Maybe we grew up hanging posters on the wall instead of fine art or portraiture. Perhaps we grew up hearing common stereotypes and assumptions about affluent people. Even if you've been serving an affluent clientele for years or decades, a change of perspective can help us drop long-held assumptions and open us up to a whole new way of seeing. As is often said, if you want to see different results, you have to see things differently.

In all my work as a coach and author, I favor an inside-out approach. We often have to start with a mindset shift to get the results we want. However, in this case, it's not so much about thinking differently. It's about *seeing* differently. The broader philosophies about the luxury market shared in this element are intended to help you see differently.

Seeing differently involves shifting perspectives and being open to new viewpoints and understandings. Much like a photographer who adjusts their angle to capture an image from a fresh perspective, we too can shift our viewpoint to gain a new understanding. It's about being open to experiences beyond our usual perspective and challenging assumptions that can limit us.

When you don't come from the same world as others and are fed stereotypes and misinformation, it can be all too easy to adopt assumptions. Believe me, I heard all the assumptions about "rich people" growing up. They're difficult, their children are raised by nannies, money can't buy happiness, etc. Holding onto assumptions is so dangerous in serving the luxury clientele because they are so highly perceptive. Imagine if you felt like people only wanted you for your money, wouldn't you be put off? I'll share a pivotal moment I experienced early in my career.

I had recently photographed the children of one of my very first high-end clients, let's call her Mrs. K. We met outside at a table beside the pool looking out at the lawn and gardens of the sprawling estate for me to show her proofs of the portraits I had taken. She made her selections, which included dozens of 8"x10" and 5"x7" portraits of various poses, many duplicates of the same pose. When done with her selections, she invited me to complete the invoice and she would return shortly. I was served iced-tea and some finger sandwiches and went about the task of adding up what was going to be a huge order. By far, the largest to date for me. Around $50,000.

Shortly after, her assistant came and collected the invoice, presumably to return with a check. Instead, I saw Mrs. K walking down the winding walkway and steps from the grand terrace. She was a powerful woman and even from a distance I could tell this was not going to go well.

She laid the invoice down on the table in front of me and said, "Young man, I know what's going on here. Rework your invoice and try again." With that, she walked away.

I was stumped at first. What had I done wrong? I followed my standard pricing structure. $300 for each 8"x 10", $250 for each 5"x 7". She had chosen multiple copies of many different poses. But then I put myself in her shoes. I imagined she wondered why she was paying the same price for the third, fifth, and tenth, portrait of the same pose as the first. Even though, in the pre-digital era, each small portrait was in fact custom, from her perspective, she was looking for something else. On the spot, I reworked the invoice, charging full price for the first and discounting the additional versions of the same pose, reducing the amount almost by half. Believe me, it was still a very substantial profit and I felt very compensated for my creativity and effort.

Her assistant returned once again, whisked the invoice away but this time she returned with a check, paid in full. Mrs. K and I went on to work together for many years, always with a relationship of tremendous respect.

She called me out. Her radar was up and she wanted to be treated fairly. I imagined she was looking to pay for what felt like fair compensation overall and not itemized products. She was focused on the relationship, not the products and I respected that. I also realized, of course, in luxury you are creating bespoke products and experiences and sometimes standard pricing and procedures don't apply. You can always assume your clients will not let you get away with a single thing. But here's also what's important to notice. She gave me a second chance and for that I am deeply grateful. If I had been asked to leave that would have shattered my confidence. But she didn't. I trust she felt my good intention and gave me a chance to grow, to rise up to the occasion, to respond to a call of greatness.

Any assumptions or judgments you may have or holding steadfast to your own ways can be blocks to understanding and empathy, and can cause you to jump to inaccurate conclusions, and let's admit it, we see more of what we believe to be true. It's why I prefer to refer to the clients we seek to serve as deserving, not discerning. It's not that they are not discerning, by definition, they are. Meaning, yes, they have high standards. But the word discerning often carries with it an air of judgment, more like picky. What if instead we believe they deserve the high standards they are asking for instead of assuming they are just being picky? I believe this changes how we think about our clients, makes us more empathetic, and our clients feel that. The powerful awareness of the energy of words creates a change of perspective.

In practical terms, seeing differently often means stepping into someone else's shoes, especially when it's a world you don't come from. A willingness to walk in someone else's shoes is a choice to approach situations with open-mindedness, curiosity, and setting aside pre-conceived notions.

When we see differently, we can spot connections, resources, or opportunities that our previous perspective may have otherwise missed. Seeing differently can allow us to recognize beauty, complexity, or value where we previously saw only obstacles or limitations. This openness can reframe our thinking and lead to solutions or ideas that genuinely surprise us. This is important for some of the creative solutions that are necessary to stand out and be exceptional in the world of luxury. Seeing differently helps unlock opportunities that conventional thinking might miss.

This Element on Luxury Philosophies is an invitation to step back and look at the luxury market in a broader context. To look at the challenges facing luxury in a mass-marketed world, the exceptionally high standard it takes to stand out, and the lasting legacy of luxury. All of these I believe will put you in a different position to value your clients and develop creative ideas to make you and your business be exceptional and stand out as such.

For as long as there's an opportunity to see things differently, there's an opportunity for things to be different. I stand by that as my eternal hope for the future.

CARTIER
The Importance of Legacy

CARTIER, "THE JEWELER OF KINGS and the king of jewelers," has cultivated a legacy of elegance, prestige, and artistry since its founding in 1847. This brand history is embodied in its connection to icons like Grace Kelly, whose timelessness personified Cartier's design philosophy.

In 1956, Hollywood star Grace Kelly became Princess Grace of Monaco, epitomizing grace and sophistication. For their royal engagement, Prince Rainier III gifted her a Cartier ring featuring a 10.48-carat emerald-cut diamond—an emblem of understated luxury. Grace's relationship with Cartier extended beyond jewelry. She became a muse of sorts, blending Hollywood glamour with European aristocracy. The Cartier pieces she was often seen wearing—from diamond necklaces to Art Deco brooches—symbolized style and taste. To this day, Monaco continues to honor Princess Grace, and her connection to Cartier remains unmistakable, making Cartier and Monaco also interwoven.

Cartier's genius lies in storytelling. Through archival exhibitions like Cartier and Women, it celebrates iconic figures like Grace Kelly and Elizabeth Taylor, intertwining its heritage with theirs. These connections reinforce Cartier's story that its creations are heirlooms and cultural milestones, not mere luxury items.

By embracing its storied history, Cartier has built more than a brand—it has crafted a multi-generational cultural legacy. To wear Cartier is to carry a lineage of elegance and to belong to an enduring tradition of artistry and refinement. Cartier magnificently engages their consumers in their story, making the buyer feel part of a long lineage, past and future.

RAISING THE BAR

Business Interactions as Life-Transforming Events

HAVE YOU EVER HAD A day that wasn't going so well, maybe challenges at home or stress at work, and you walked into your local coffee shop and the familiar barista brightened your mood with a smile and your preferred drink prepared to your liking, ready to go?

Or have you had a day going perfectly well until you had to call customer service of a tech company or bank, and your entire vibe shifted from delightful to disaster?

Now imagine a world where every interaction with a business leaves you not just satisfied, but meaningfully changed for the better. In this world, businesses aim to make every transaction, service, and product purchase a life-transforming event for their customers. This ambitious goal would revolutionize the very nature of business, creating profound, positive impacts on people's lives.

Does it seem like a tall order? A pipe dream? Perhaps. However, I believe luxury brands and services are uniquely qualified to set a new standard of doing business. Already keenly aware of higher standards, attention to detail, exceptional service, and deep knowledge of their customers, it's just another notch up to imagine business transactions as life-transforming events. Besides, why not aim for the ultimate so that even if a business falls a bit short, the standards of service have still transcended the norm.

As the world becomes increasingly dependent on technology, consumers will be looking not only to take care of their day-to-day business interactions but also for periodic excursions that feel like more than just a purchase or transaction. They will need humanity, interaction, socialization, and the assurance that overall the world is still a great place and humans are basically good. Does all this sound too noble? Too dramatic?

For many, the purchase of luxury goods and services is a departure from the norm. The customer may have saved up for this experience or perhaps it's part of a holiday getaway with increased pressure to have a great adventure. For others, interacting with luxury brands and services may be typical, but with an epidemic of loneliness in the world, the interaction with a sales associate or service provider has significant emotional importance.

It may be a tall order or high calling, but I don't think it's hard to imagine that what exceptional luxury brands and services will need to do in the future will go beyond excellence to creating life-transforming moments for their customers.

How might we accomplish this?

PERSONALIZED CUSTOMER EXPERIENCES

IN THIS VISIONARY LANDSCAPE, BUSINESSES would place an unprecedented emphasis on understanding their customers at an even deeper, personal level. The very same technology that can create impersonalization would be employed to gather deeply personal insights not just about purchasing habits, but about personal aspirations, challenges, lifestyle, and dreams. For example, I recently purchased some sneakers at a luxury brand in Paris. Within minutes of my purchase, I received a text from my normal sales associate of the same brand in the U.S. wishing me a wonderful vacation in Paris. Clearly, their entire worldwide system was integrated so she knew when I made a purchase elsewhere. Of course, she expressed her hope I'd come to see her at her location sometime soon. I didn't mind her wanting to maintain my business. I have every intention of doing so anyway. But to receive her message and know she sees my devotion to the brand was a delight. Technology can be used to create an unbelievably personal experience if used as such and each customer interaction would become an opportunity to uplift and inspire.

HOLISTIC WELL-BEING

I ONCE HAD A CONVERSATION on my podcast, The Self-Employed Life, with a technology investor and futurist about the impact of AI. We spoke about businesses and industries that could be negatively impacted by the proliferation of AI as well as which industries will benefit. He predicts that businesses committed to transforming lives—that focus on well-being, personal growth, and happiness—will see incredible growth. Coaching, nutrition, fitness, and healthcare as well as exceptional culinary experiences. Fitness centers might offer integrated programs combining physical exercise, mental health support, and nutritional guidance, ensuring that members leave each session feeling invigorated and supported in all aspects of their lives. The food industry will explore new ways to produce cleaner food and dining out will be an enriching and fulfilling escape. The bottom line is businesses and industries that transform people's lives will flourish as the world becomes more reliant on technology.

COMMUNITY BUILDING

IN THIS WORLD OF LIFE-TRANSFORMING business, companies would serve as hubs for community building, creating opportunities where customers can connect, share experiences, and support one another. Going beyond just the local cafe, many types of businesses might host events that bring together diverse groups for meaningful dialogue and collaboration. Luxury brands could go beyond the sales events and bring their customers together for an evening of connection, an opportunity to socialize with people who at least have one thing in common—their love for the brand. Undoubtedly, such like-minded people will likely find many more things in common and therefore build enriching relationships. Brands can also create online communities where users share stories of transformation, providing inspiration and encouragement to others. One just needs to join a travel group on Facebook to see how much people enjoy sharing something they have in common.

MEASURING IMPACT

FINALLY, THESE BUSINESSES WOULD ESTABLISH metrics to measure their impact on customers' lives, and not just the money. They would track and report on how their products and services contribute to customers' well-being, personal growth, community development, and creating a sustainable world. In a seeming paradox, I favor a data-driven approach to how you are emotionally changing people's lives. Measuring intangible impact increases awareness and ensures continuous improvement and accountability to drive further innovations, enhancements, and efforts.

◆ IN THE END...

IF LUXURY GOODS AND SERVICES made it their goal to be leaders in the quest to transform the lives of their customers, the business world would become a force for exciting positive change. Every interaction would be an opportunity to be life-transforming, creating a ripple effect that extends far beyond luxury.

FORGING YOUR OWN PATH IN A MASS-MARKETED WORLD

In a world dominated by mass marketing and standardized customer experiences, luxury brands have always had to defy norms to maintain their unique identity and appeal. With most conversation and information geared toward mass-marketed business, luxury businesses can be left feeling "unspoken to."

When speaking to event planners who aren't sure if they have a large enough segment of attendees who are reaching the luxury market, I point out that they might be surprised at how many people come out of the woodwork. It's because in a mass-marketed—and for that matter, a mass conversation world—those appealing to the high-end often need to peer in from the outside to see what can apply in their business and what needs to be completely disregarded.

Let's look at a few areas of conversation typically geared toward mass-market businesses but where you can extract and adapt some important lessons.

QUALITY AND SERVICE

At the heart of luxury lies a commitment to quality and service while mass-market brands prioritize efficiency and cost-effectiveness. Such dedication to attention to detail in quality and service not only sets luxury brands apart from their mass-market counterparts but also reinforces their aura of exclusivity and prestige.

However, the speed at which mass-marketed businesses operate can have a significant effect on customer expectations, even from luxury brands committed to only providing the highest quality.

Luxury businesses need to figure out how to deliver both: a commitment to the highest standards of quality and speed to meet the expectations for today's luxury buyers. I recently ordered a beautiful hand-made umbrella with a custom monogram engraved on the handle from a small family-owned company in Italy called Il Marchesato. From date of order to delivery to my home in the U.S. was five days. As I've shared my latest acquisition with great pride, I have always stressed not only the obvious beauty and craftsmanship of the umbrella but also the speed of delivery of such a high-quality item. Luxury brands need to recognize it's a "yes, and" world for today's consumers. Consumers want the same high standard of quality and exceptional level and speed of service.

INNOVATION AND TECHNOLOGY

WHEREAS MASS-MARKET BRANDS CAN BE quick to implement the latest technology into customer experiences, luxury brands have to do so with a bit more caution. The technology itself might be the latest trend, but luxury brands sets trends, not follow them. A luxury business then needs to consider where they can uniquely add to common technology. It might be the same technology a mass-market business uses but needs to feel different and provide an elevated user experience. Virtual reality may be similar across the board. But what the luxury buyer and mass-marketed buyer experience when using virtual reality must feel different.

Integrating what will become common technologies in uncommon ways may be one of the biggest challenges put before luxury brands to separate themselves from mass-marketed businesses in years to come.

DIGITAL MARKETING AND SOCIAL MEDIA

LUXURY BRANDS MUST ALSO NAVIGATE the increasingly complex landscape of digital marketing and social media. While mass-market brands can leverage influencers and paid advertisements to reach a broad audience, luxury brands must tread carefully to maintain their aura of exclusivity and sophistication. This often requires a delicate balance between engaging with consumers on social media platforms and preserving the mystique and allure that have long been synonymous with the luxury category.

There's a scene in the Netflix series, Emily in Paris, where Sylvie, the head of the fictitious marketing agency Savoir explains the difference between American marketing and French luxury marketing to Emily with a dismissive wave of her hand, "That's the problem, you have no mystery."

There's some truth to that and a real challenge for luxury brands. There's no stopping the fast-moving train of digital marketing and social media. Transparency is expected and behind-the-scenes content is compelling. But how to do so without losing the allure of mystery and intrigue that luxury brands have for so long relied on is the challenge.

◆ IN THE END...

WITH EVEN THESE FEW EXAMPLES, we can see that the majority of conversations in the world of business have always been primarily for mass-marketed businesses. The need for luxury brands and businesses to pay attention to what's happening in the mass-marketed world and make it their own while continuing to be steadfast in maintaining their positioning in the luxury space may be greater than ever. The force of mediocrity is strong. The desire for fast and easy over best in class can easily become a simplistic choice for consumers. Once again, luxury brands are called to maintain their position as the keepers of standards.

BUILDING A SMALL LUXURY BUSINESS IN A BIG LUXURY BRAND WORLD

It's impossible to talk about luxury without referencing the most popular luxury brands—Louis Vuitton, Dior, Gucci, etc. As a coach, author, and keynote speaker for independent luxury providers such as interior designers, home builders, jewelry makers, artists, and other services, I am keenly aware that referencing these large luxury brands may not feel relatable to the small business owner or solo service provider. Rightfully so.

While much can be learned from large luxury brands, the strategies for small luxury businesses are different and the challenges are unique. Notice how I intentionally referenced large luxury "brands" and small luxury "businesses." More on that in a moment.

Whether you are a small business with many employees, a small team, or a business of one, let's discuss the common challenges and solutions of being a small luxury business in a big luxury brand world.

BRAND AWARENESS AND CREDIBILITY

In the luxury market, reputation is everything. Large brands have the advantage of long-established history and credibility, while smaller luxury businesses often struggle to gain recognition and trust from affluent consumers. Building a reputation in the luxury market takes time and consistent effort and small brands may find it difficult to get noticed.

Solution: For one, start thinking big even if you're going to stay small. All those recognizable luxury names you can think of have built a luxury "brand." To succeed in the luxury market, you need to understand you may be building a small business because you are not trying to compete on size, but you need to develop a strong luxury Brand (with a capital B). The luxury buyer is buying into a brand, an image, and a reputation.

No matter your product or service, you need to establish your brand as the best choice in the marketplace. You don't have to compete with international luxury brands. Just build the best brand story and image that dominates your industry in the market size of your choice—local, regional, or national. Lastly, while it may take longer to build the luxury brand you want, you have to come out of the gate established as the best. Luxury is not something you can level up to. If you start being seen as mainstream, it's nearly impossible to ever be seen as upscale. Establish the standards by which you'll operate, understand the needs of your ideal customer, build a clear luxury brand, put in consistent and unwavering effort, and be patient. It's worth the wait.

ACCESS TO BIG DATA AND CONSUMER INSIGHTS

In business today and especially in luxury, it can seem like data is king. Large luxury brands have access to sophisticated data analytics and market research that allow them to precisely target their ideal customers. They can analyze purchasing trends, identify emerging markets, track social media behavior and personalize their offerings to a much higher degree. Small luxury businesses, on the other hand, often lack the resources to gather this level of data, leaving them seemingly in the dark about who their customers are and their behaviors.

Solution: Utilize the data available, study the actions of larger luxury brands, and apply what I refer to as a filter of discernment. Take the best from what you can learn, toss out the rest, and leverage your advantages. For starters, a small business can use cost-effective tools such as social media analytics, Google Analytics, and customer feedback surveys. These data points can offer valuable insights into customer preferences, behaviors, and trends that can help small businesses tailor their offerings and marketing strategies.

Additionally, small luxury businesses can engage in direct communication with their clientele to gain first-hand insights in ways that larger brands may struggle to do. This direct interaction is an advantage that smaller brands can capitalize on, allowing them to develop deeper and more personalized relationships with their customers. Also, use the power of observation. Small businesses often have opportunities to observe the behavior and lifestyle of their clients in ways that large brands could only dream of. This front-row seat is priceless.

I stand by a core belief that the best data will never hold up against real-life in-the-moment encounters with the luxury buyer to fully understand their worlds and adjust as needed at a moment's notice. Intimacy is the greatest secret weapon of small business brands.

LIMITED MARKETING BUDGETS

MARKETING IS THE LIFEBLOOD OF any business, but luxury marketing, in particular, comes with a high price tag. Large luxury brands invest millions of dollars into slick advertising campaigns, celebrity endorsements, and global events. They have the financial means to create experiences that capture the imaginations of consumers. For small luxury brands, limited marketing budgets make it difficult to compete on the same scale.

Solution: Small luxury brands should focus on more specific marketing strategies, targeting the segments of the luxury market where they can make the most impact. Smaller businesses can invest in in-person, digital, and low-tech strategies that offer more precise targeting and build stronger relationships. For example, maintaining a high repeat business percentage can cost nearly nothing through email marketing and personal emails. Often, a simple reminder email to reengage a past customer is all it takes. Relationships are the currency and require the least amount of money invested. As I say when coaching small luxury brands, make it impossible for people to break up with you. Many of the most effective strategies to re-engage past customers and attract new customers require effort and relationship building much more than money.

LACK OF SUPPORT

LARGE LUXURY BRANDS ENJOY THE dual advantages of being among the chosen few for their customers and of standing alongside a rather large group of businesses that dominate the industry. This provides them with an abundance of resources and available data. For small luxury businesses, this can be an isolating experience. When you're a small luxury brand, by definition you are not like others in your field. You are the exception. While this is ideal and intentional for brand building, it can also be a lonely experience with far fewer resources and peer groups available.

Solution: Consider connecting with and spending more time with luxury providers outside of your industry. By being exceptional in your field, there will be few others that you can relate to, so you'll need to expand your sphere. Additionally, it offers great opportunity for cross innovation amongst luxury providers and can open up creative marketing and service ideas.

Also, take the best of what you can learn from large luxury brands and creatively apply ideas in ways that fit a small business. Lastly, small businesses need to more readily ask for what they need. Understand that by not being for everyone, you're going to have to dig deeper for the resources you'll need as well as the skillsets and strategies that you'll want to learn. There are simply not as many resources available for luxury brands and marketers. A search in Amazon will provide you with countless general business books with a very small, tiny, percentage being for luxury businesses. You will have to look deeper, reach further, and be clearer on what you need to gain the support you desire.

◆ IN THE END...

SMALL LUXURY BUSINESSES CAN ABSOLUTELY overcome the challenges and thrive in a world dominated by large brands and big data in the luxury industry. In fact, small, highly personalized, and intimate are the epitome of luxury and perhaps the enviable goal of the large brands. Embracing creative marketing strategies, building a strong brand identity, and keeping a close eye on customer behavior are crucial for succeeding in this competitive space.

LANSON CHAMPAGNE
The Luxury of Understated Excellence

IN THE WORLD OF LUXURY champagne, Lanson occupies a fascinating position. It's not as famous as Veuve Clicquot, yet it thrives as a brand of choice for those who appreciate quiet sophistication. Lanson has found strength in being a connoisseur's brand—a second-tier choice that prides itself on excellence rather than popularity.

The brand also benefits from its understated branding and royal connection. As the official champagne of the British Royal Family, Lanson exudes a heritage of refinement. They avoid flashy marketing, focusing instead on unique quality and personal experiences. This subtle approach appeals to buyers who favor quiet luxury over common choice.

Lanson champagne deliberately and distinctively rejects malolactic fermentation, a process most champagne houses use to soften acidity. By preserving the wine's natural freshness, Lanson creates champagne with vibrant liveliness and exceptional bubbles. This unique production decision gives its champagne a distinct profile, earning respect from those who value craftsmanship and originality over mass-market appeal.

Lanson's positioning as a "less obvious" choice is an intentional strategy and one I favored as well when choosing the location of my photography gallery. I avoided the obvious choice on the prestigious avenue and opted for a side street. That location connoted a found treasure that was there for the residents, not visitors.

Strategic second-tier positioning embodies the idea that true luxury isn't always the loudest. In an era where popularity often means predictability, Lanson's quieter success proves that understated excellence holds enduring power.

KEY QUESTIONS TO ASK WHEN SERVING THE LUXURY MARKET

THE FOLLOWING QUESTIONS ARE REAL, practical, and common questions I often receive from attendees at my speaking engagements. Since they are essential and relatable questions for anyone looking to successfully serve affluent clients, I've gathered them here for your consideration.

Q: If you don't come from their world, how can you relate to one another?

Working with luxury clients often means stepping into an entirely different world, one that might feel far removed from your own upbringing and lifestyle. But here's the key: they aren't looking for you to be like them. Instead, they're drawn to professionals who are completely focused on delivering what you're great at and fully committed to excellence without pretense. In my experience, affluent clients respect ambition, drive, and dedication to service without any consideration of whether you live like them. You have to maintain a moderate degree of decorum, but they don't expect you to be like them.

For example, I used to work with many hotel concierges at the nicest hotels in New York City. They would often refer clients visiting from other countries who wanted family portraits in Central Park or were celebrating a special occasion while in the city. The best concierges at high-end hotels are known for their elegance, courtesy, and unparalleled service. Yet, at the end of their shift, they return to modest apartments in New York City, living lives that are far from the luxury of the hotels they work for. What makes these concierges exceptional is not their similarity to their clients but their commitment to providing a first-class experience. Similarly, in my career as a photographer, there were times I had to crawl under dining tables to motivate a child to come out from hiding or make silly noises to get their attention during shoots. Luxury clients aren't impressed by pretentiousness but by results. First and foremost, they want to see dedication, expertise, and presence. So, honestly, don't worry about it. Be yourself.

Q: How do you go about pricing your services in the luxury market?

Pricing is an art form in the luxury market. For high-end clients, pricing is about perception, value, and simplicity. Affluent customers aren't interested in "discount psychology"—that's for mainstream buyers. Instead, round numbers like $500 or $2000 resonate more than "$499" or "$1999," which can come across as gimmicky or too calculated. Rounded pricing suggests confidence and transparency.

For luxury clients, price is often a reflection of value and trust. They expect prices to align with quality, but they don't want to feel they're paying more than necessary. For instance, additional travel, lodging expenses, or little extra fees can feel like unnecessary surcharges if they're itemized too specifically. As one of my clients said to me about my $1000 session fee, "In comparison to what I spend on all the portraits, it feels like a tax." Meaning, it felt like this small amount added to a large investment. I understood that and would often drop the session fee after a few years of working with a client. You want to keep their focus on the big picture of the amazing experience and exceptional value they are receiving. Perhaps consider an all-inclusive pricing structure or just build it in which creates clarity and avoids the perception of being "nickeled and dimed." Similarly, if you're offering an on-location service, consider a minimum fee that assures you that your time will be sufficiently compensated and absorbs all the extra fees without overly itemizing the charges.

Luxury buyers value ease and convenience. They appreciate transparent, straightforward pricing that respects their time and reflects the quality of what they're paying for. Yes, they are very detail-oriented but do them and yourself a favor and don't get too detailed about pricing.

Q: How did you get started and break through to the luxury market?

Breaking into the luxury market is about strategically building relationships and positioning yourself where your ideal affluent clients might find you or be introduced to you. My approach to establishing myself as a luxury portrait photographer was rooted in the idea of letting the right people know I existed, without ever asking for anything in return. I used to say to myself—and now tell my coaching clients—just let as many of the right people as you can find know you exist.

Starting out, I consistently visited upscale children's boutiques, high-end toy stores, and coveted country clubs, not to make sales pitches, but simply to introduce myself to the people who managed these places. I used to walk around with a long black architectural tube, one where you would store rolled up blueprints back in the day, with samples of my portraits inside. It was such an odd thing to carry people would often ask about what was in tube. Before they barely finished asking, I was already pulling out my work. I never asked for anything or suggested they refer anyone to me. I met my goal to simply let as many people as possible know I existed. This led to many beneficial relationships that did lead to referrals.

This approach might seem passive, but it's subtle, non-intrusive, and perfect for the luxury market. I suppose you could call it networking but I reframed it as simply letting people know I existed and being open to whatever happened. I think it was the looseness of it all that worked. As has been said, a clenched fist can't receive. This was all just very open. It requires patience and a genuine interest in connecting with people without an immediate payoff. Luxury clients and other professionals in the luxury space often value subtlety and authenticity in relationships; they don't always respond well to overt marketing. When your presence is known and your reputation precedes you, affluent clients and your referral sources will feel more comfortable reaching out because the connection feels natural and built on mutual respect.

Q: What's the best way to communicate value to affluent clients?

Affluent clients are typically less interested in specific features of a service and more focused on the impact it will have on their lives. Communicating value effectively in this market means emphasizing outcomes and experiences. Rather than discussing the number of hours or specific details of a package, focus on the benefits they'll experience and how your service will meet their unique needs.

For example, as a portrait photographer, instead of outlining session lengths or wardrobe changes, I might focus on how the photos will capture family memories in a timeless way, ready to be passed down through generations. How much their kids will appreciate that they captured their childhood when they are older. Affluent clients want to feel assured that they're investing in something with lasting value. Highlight the impact, not the logistics.

This approach shifts the conversation from technicalities to a story about the transformation or the impact of your work. Luxury buyers are often willing to pay a premium when they feel they're getting something customized and tailored to them. So, make it clear that your service or product offers not just quality but a meaningful, memorable, or even transformative experience.

Q: How do you handle expectations in the luxury market?

Managing expectations in the luxury market requires transparency, clear boundaries, and a touch of finesse. Affluent clients can have high and specific expectations, and it's essential to be upfront about what's possible. Set clear parameters from the start, and if they request additional services or modifications, address these proactively. Not meeting expectations can be disastrous so be clear and realistic. Under promise and over-deliver, even though they may try to convince you otherwise in the beginning. Be strong and maintain your boundaries. It will pay off for you later. Be careful that you don't try to over-serve, and the client is definitely not always right.

One of the keys to managing expectations is communication. Make it a priority to keep clients updated throughout your engagement, especially if there are any changes or adjustments needed along the way. Affluent clients want to feel in control and informed without having to micromanage. By keeping them involved and updating them regularly, you can prevent misunderstandings and build trust.

Additionally, remember that luxury clients value time as much as quality. Delivering on time or even slightly early is a powerful way to exceed expectations. By doing so, you demonstrate reliability, which is a quality they deeply respect and unfortunately often rare.

◆ IN THE END...

IF I WERE TO SUMMARIZE the common thread in these answers, they all have to do with being present. Fully present in service and not letting anything cloud the act of service and what you are there to accomplish. No pretentiousness, no silly pricing, and cutting straight through create the best possible relationships.

THE ENDURING STRENGTH OF LUXURY BRANDS

A Beacon of Hope in Turbulent Times

I'VE READ MUCH OVER THE years about the potential decline of the luxury market. Well-known brands are seemingly at risk, with affluent consumers opting for discount retailers, the changing values of today's consumers, and concerns over the economy.

Maybe it's because I've been in business for forty years and have seen many other changes in the market. Or perhaps it's simply that I feel as consumers often feel—we want our luxury brands to succeed. They hold a special place in our lives and the world. Perhaps a look at the resilience and history of the luxury market will help us appreciate luxury's ability to stay relevant and feel confident in its future.

Luxury brands represent more than just high-end products and services. They stand as symbols of hope, extraordinary quality, high standards, and timelessness. Their resilience in the face of adversity is not just a testament to their brand but to the values they embody and the promise of a better tomorrow.

THE RESILIENCE OF LUXURY BRANDS

THROUGHOUT HISTORY, LUXURY BRANDS AND services have withstood economic downturns, global conflicts, and drastic cultural changes. Whether it was the Great Depression, World War II, the 2008 financial crisis, or the COVID-19 pandemic, many luxury brands emerged not only intact but stronger than ever.

Fashion houses such as Chanel and Dior exemplify this resilience. Chanel was founded during a time of tremendous social change in 1910 when Coco Chanel introduced simple yet elegant fashion as women stepped out of their traditional domestic roles and into the workforce. The House of Dior is often credited with saving the fashion industry and bringing Paris back to life with Christian Dior's noble promise to make women feel beautiful again.

Luxury automotive brands like Rolls-Royce and Bentley have remained synonymous with excellence for more than a century, despite world wars and economic hardships. These brands thrived because they stayed true to their core values of engineering brilliance, craftsmanship, and a sense of rarity.

These brands became symbols of perseverance and aspiration, offering hope and a promise that we can and will endure.

A DEDICATION TO QUALITY AND CRAFTSMANSHIP

THE VERY ESSENCE OF LUXURY is built on unwavering dedication to quality, service, exclusivity, and an exceptional experience. In times of uncertainty, people look for products and services that will last. Luxury brands meet that need in ways mass-produced goods cannot. Luxury services offer a much-needed respite from challenging times—and products in this category offer consumers much-needed indulgence and break from reality.

In times of crisis, consumers will often take a more careful approach to what they buy. They seek to buy fewer, but better, items that will last. In a rapidly changing world, these brands offer a sense of permanence—something rare in a consumerism-driven, throwaway world.

When the world is unpredictable, people gravitate toward stability. Luxury items, with their promise of longevity and value, offer exactly that.

ADAPTATION AND INNOVATION

THE RESILIENCE OF LUXURY BRANDS does not come from stubbornly sticking to old ways but from a unique ability to innovate while staying true to core values. Luxury brands have evolved with changing times by incorporating technology, embracing sustainability, and responding to new consumer needs, all while maintaining the same level of excellence in quality and design.

Brands like Gucci and Prada have taken on digital transformation, adapting their presence to virtual environments and even using augmented reality to create new luxury experiences. Brands like Cartier have taken on initiatives in support of environmental causes, healthcare, and education, creating a direct connection between luxury and social good.

At the same time, these brands stay rooted in the tradition of craftsmanship and exclusivity. The future of luxury is about seamlessly combining innovation with the time-honored values that have always defined it.

BEACONS OF HOPE

BEYOND MATERIAL WORTH, LUXURY BRANDS represent emotional security. In a chaotic world, luxury goods and services often serve as an emotional anchor, a reminder that some things remain constant. In an ever-changing world, luxury brands also offer aspirations and dreams. They represent not just the life we have, but the life we want. In hard times, they offer a vision of hope and a connection to a better, more beautiful future. For many, purchasing a luxury item is not just a transaction but an affirmation of deserving and an investment in joy, providing a sense of escape and personal reward in a way that's far more intimate and emotional than other purchases.

◆ IN THE END...

THROUGHOUT HISTORY, IN TIMES FILLED with uncertainty and rapid change, luxury brands have continued to serve as beacons of hope. They provide stability and comfort by offering something that transcends the craziness of the world. Timeless elegance, unparalleled quality, a commitment to excellence, and a piece of good or joy that will outlast the challenging times. As the world faces new challenges, economic downturns, climate change, and global unrest, luxury brands stand as a reminder that while trends and circumstances may shift, certain values remain—like hope, beauty, quality, and craftsmanship—and will always have a place in the world.

ELEMENT II

Luxury Service Mindset

The most powerful way to connect and serve is by showing up as yourself—fully, authentically, and confidently.

LUXURY SERVICE MINDSET
Introduction

MANY CONVERSATIONS ABOUT MINDSET SHIFTS reduce the concept to a few surface-level "positive thinking" techniques. Don't get me wrong. I'm a fan of positive thinking and when I photographed Norman Vincent Peale, the author of the classic book that may have started it all, *The Power of Positive Thinking,* it was one of the highest honors of my photography career. But, this simple "shift" idea is often dramatically oversimplified. Effectively serving an affluent clientele demands more than a quick change of attitude for you to continuously grow and be authentic. It requires a deeper, ongoing process of rewiring your brain, continually overcoming obvious and non-obvious blocks, and making more fundamental shifts in thinking. I prefer to look at it as a mindset evolution rather than a shift. It's about you growing into your greatness. And truly, where you start in life has nothing to do with where you end up.

Since we're talking about mindset, let me go all woo-woo on you for a moment. There is an intended sequence, a flow, to this Element. It mirrors how I believe you go from where you are to where you want to be. It's not a one-time thing or snap-decision shift but rather a continual, circular process of progress. It goes something like this:

Become aware of a new way of thinking, face the obstacles that come with change, clear the path, set the stage, and be pulled towards the results you want.

Yes, be pulled, because once the circumstances are in place, it's as if you are pulled toward your goals. It's an environment for change and growth. The information in this Element reflects this sequence for the desired result: creating change within yourself to prepare you to serve this clientele.

This is about changing your internal wiring, you could say. We can refer to it as thinking differently but I believe it's more than that. It's about creating the change that makes this way of thinking natural. Mindset shifts at this level are less about simply "thinking differently" and more about closing gaps that come from your background, removing limiting beliefs that may unknowingly influence how you think, and creating your own sense of belonging in situations that may initially feel foreign or intimidating.

Let's further address the idea of feeling like you belong. While this Element tackles some of the specific mindsets to adopt into our way of being, collectively it's all about belonging. I don't believe you can fully succeed in the luxury market with an "us and them" mentality. I also don't believe it's entirely about being accepted as a means of feeling like you belong. The sense of belonging has to come from within yourself. Serving this clientele should feel like the most natural place for you to be—and that's what you're working toward. Your sense of belonging will exude confidence and comfort: two very appealing traits in all segments of business.

The challenge is you may be carrying internal blocks such as imposter syndrome, self-doubt, or a feeling that you don't truly "belong" in these circles. Many luxury service providers came from humble beginnings, and when stepping into spaces with clients who have access to immense wealth, it's easy to be intimidated or feel like an outsider. But here's the truth and I wholeheartedly believe this: It's not about trying to fit in or earning someone else's acceptance. It's about cultivating a deep knowing of your intrinsic value and being confident about the level at which you deliver. This is what leads to the feeling of belonging. You deserve to serve people who value your uniqueness, craftsmanship, and passion, versus tiptoeing around like a timid outsider.

True success in serving an affluent clientele comes from embracing who you are and standing firmly in what you offer. The most powerful way to connect and serve is by showing up as yourself—fully, authentically, and confidently. When you're grounded in your values, and clear on the unique value you bring, you start to realize that clients aren't looking for someone like them. They're looking for someone who offers genuine value and brings something different, even refreshing, to the table.

Don't seek acceptance or try to fit in. Instead, claim your place as a trusted expert. Not only will this build a more authentic, lasting relationship with your clients, but it will also strengthen your confidence and sense of belonging in the luxury world. You're there because you're great at what you do and you're well-intended. Trust that's enough. You're enough.

Lastly, the word deserving is tossed around a lot in luxury circles, often with an air of arrogance. So, here's a mindset shift I'd like you to consider as you round out this Element. Let's flip the script from your clients solely getting what they deserve because of the excellence you provide to you also getting all that you deserve. If you welcome the idea that you should receive in life all that you deserve, it will make it easier for you to understand where your clients are coming from. Perhaps they are not acting entitled as often accused but rather they are uncannily comfortable with receiving what they deserve.

Feelings of deserving are a pulling mechanism, drawing you toward all that is available for you. What if everything you want in life is already there? Only blocks stand between where you are and having it all, and once cleared, everything you deserve is there.

The most grounded affluent people I ever met were very comfortable with themselves and with what they have. As if they were comfortable in getting what they deserved. It often allowed them to be very grateful but also not entirely surprised at their good fortune.

This Element asks you to do some work on yourself and to think differently. In doing so, you may not only find yourself more confident and at ease but will also come to see that as where you truly belong. And don't be entirely surprised if, as a result, you get all that you deserve.

THE MINDSET GAP THAT CAN
KEEP YOU FROM SUCCESS

This might sound obvious, but it's a principle many luxury service providers and business owners unintentionally overlook and it's one of the biggest mindset blocks:

You can't serve the luxury market and shop at the Dollar Store.

Of course, you *can*. Maybe. Sometimes. What I'm referring to is the challenge you're putting yourself in if you're focused on saving money and cutting corners while you're trying to get others to spend money and appreciate only the best. While the Dollar Store reference may seem exaggerated, the concept is highly relevant when it comes to aligning your mindset and actions with the clientele you aim to serve.

Let's dive into the critical role this dissonance plays in causing the gap between where you are and where you want to be when serving the luxury market, how it's keeping you from the success you seek, and what you can do about it.

THE MINDSET GAP

Here's the real issue: You're asking your brain to hold two conflicting truths. On one hand, you expect your clients to pay top dollar for your products and services. On the other hand, you're prioritizing discounts and DIY solutions in your own business and life. This creates a mental tug of war. One side pulls you toward the potential for success and an abundant mindset, while the other drags you back, reinforcing scarcity and limitations.

This internal conflict doesn't just stall your progress, it actively undermines your confidence and can encourage feelings of being an imposter.

Success in the luxury market isn't just about skill and quality. It's also about having a mindset that aligns with the clientele you serve. The wider the gap between your mindset and your aspirations, the harder it is to bridge.

ARE YOU WALKING YOUR TALK?

IMAGINE THESE TYPICAL BUSINESS OWNER scenarios. A luxury spa owner decides to build their own website to save money. An interior designer handles their own bookkeeping instead of hiring a professional. These examples are common, yet they reveal a disconnect. How can you expect others to indulge in your services or hire you as an expert if you're unwilling to hire experts in other fields?

Serving the luxury market requires congruence. It's not just about offering high-end services or products. It's about embodying the same values and standards you expect your clients to have. The problem isn't just about perception. It's about mindset. If you're not willing to invest in professional services, how can you expect your customers to? If you're aiming to attract clients who value premium experiences, yet you're cutting corners in your own life, you're creating a significant gap between your present reality and your aspirational future.

Now, in all fairness, that's not to say everything you need is easily affordable or that you have to shop the places your customers do. But minimizing the gap where you can with an ongoing aspiration to close the gap makes all the difference and should be the direction you're going. Awareness and intention play a big role here.

THE COST OF STAYING IN THE GAP

HERE'S WHAT MANY PEOPLE DON'T realize. The longer you remain in this mindset gap, the wider it grows. It's not just about appearances or surface-level congruence. It's about confidence and clarity. If your current reality is too far removed from the future you're working toward, your brain will struggle to believe in that vision.

Cutting corners in the present sends a message to your subconscious that your goals are unrealistic. That belief, even if subconscious, will hold you back. Conversely, investing in experiences, services, and products that reflect your desired future reinforces your belief that you belong in that world and that your business does too.

HOW TO CLOSE THE GAP WITHOUT BREAKING THE BANK

YOU DON'T HAVE TO SPEND a fortune to start aligning yourself with the luxury market. Here are some practical ways to bridge the gap:

1. **Immerse Yourself in Luxury Experiences**

   Visit upscale stores and shopping districts. You don't have to buy anything, just simply observe how the staff interacts with customers, how the spaces are designed, the pricing strategies, and how the atmosphere feels. This firsthand experience will deepen your understanding of the luxury mindset.

2. **Invest Strategically**

   Prioritize investing in areas that enhance your understanding of the luxury market. Whether it's hiring a top-tier coach, upgrading your branding, or experiencing premium services firsthand, these investments pay off in the long run. You get to see the world through the eyes of those you want to serve. Their experiences become relatable and the luxury brands they choose become familiar. If nothing else, familiarity with their world can foster better conversations instead of that awkward smiling through a grin because you have no idea what they are talking about.

3. Let Luxury Get in Your Bones

Think of this process as more than observation; it's about embodying the essence of luxury. You're not just visualizing your future, you're living it in small, manageable ways. The more you immerse yourself, the more natural and familiar it becomes. It's what I like to refer to as getting it in your bones. It's grounding for you and authentic to your customers.

4. Continuous Growth

Even after forty-plus years of serving affluent clients, I'm still learning. The luxury market evolves, and so do the opportunities to elevate your business. Whether you're just starting out or a seasoned professional, there's always room to raise the bar and expand your understanding.

Closing the mindset gap isn't a one-time effort. It's an ongoing process. The more you align your present actions with your future aspirations, the stronger your foundation becomes. Not only will this lead to greater success, but it will also make the journey far more enjoyable.

◆ IN THE END...

I UNDERSTAND WHAT IT'S LIKE to feel stuck in that gap. At twenty-three, I was a struggling portrait photographer trying to establish myself with affluent clients. I had literal holes in my shoes and more bills than income. But despite my circumstances, I was clear on where I wanted to go.

In the beginning, I reinvested every dollar I earned into aligning my lifestyle with my goals. I shopped in upscale stores, dined in fine restaurants, and immersed myself in the world my clients lived in. This wasn't indulgence, it was education. And not a bad way to get an education! I was learning how my ideal clients thought, behaved, and experienced life. More importantly, I was closing the gap in my mind between the life I had and the life I aspired to.

Serving the luxury market requires more than skill and ambition. It demands a mindset that's fully aligned with the values and expectations that you are asking of your clientele. Every time you invest in experiences or services that reflect your desired future, you're reinforcing your belief in your ability to serve at the highest level.

So, take the leap. Immerse yourself in the world your clients live in. Let it transform your imagination, your mindset, your business, and your future. And yes, have a little fun along the way. After all, what better way to grow than by enjoying the journey?

EMBODYING THE LIFESTYLE

How to Serve High-End Clients
When You Don't Come from Their World

MANY LUXURY GOODS AND SERVICE providers didn't come from the same world as those they serve. I certainly didn't. Yet I ended up being the go-to family portrait photographer for ultra-high-net-worth individuals. How is this accomplished?

"Fake it until you make it" certainly won't work as the luxury buyer is highly perceptive and values authenticity. How then does someone who didn't come from wealth, privilege, and a lavish lifestyle serve and get comfortable in the world of ultra-wealthy luxury buyers? You practice embodying the lifestyle of those you serve.

This doesn't mean you have to live in a mansion, wear designer clothes, or vacation in exotic destinations. It's about adopting a mindset and approach that align with the values and experiences of high-end clients. It's being willing to see the world through their eyes, without judgment. It's going where they currently shop and dine and noting what you see, hear, and feel to understand their world. It's not about faking it to be them but rather exercising extreme empathy and understanding by embodying their lifestyle.

Here's why embodying their lifestyle is a more powerful and sustainable approach than "fake it until you make it:"

- **It Builds True Empathy and Understanding**

  The foundation of serving luxury clients is understanding their world. Embodying their lifestyle means learning what truly matters to them, whether it's brand image, their image, quality, or time. This deep empathy allows you to anticipate their needs, cater to their desires, and serve them in ways that resonate with them. You're not just offering a service or product; you're providing an experience that aligns with their values.

- **It Creates Authentic Relationships**

  When you genuinely understand the lifestyle and mindset of luxury buyers, it becomes easier to build authentic relationships. These clients want to feel like you get them even if you don't come from their world. By embodying their values and demonstrating that you deeply understand them, you establish a strong foundation of trust. This authentic connection is invaluable in the luxury market, where customer loyalty and referrals are often based on personal relationships.

- **It Aligns Your Business with Expectations**

  Luxury buyers expect a certain level of excellence in everything they choose. By embodying their lifestyle, you'll naturally start aligning your business with the expectations of the luxury market. This means refining your brand messaging, perfecting your service, and ensuring that every detail, from marketing to presentation, meets the high standards of your clients. When you embody the luxury buyer's values, you'll consistently deliver an experience that reflects their expectations.

- **It Inspires Confidence and Competence**

  Instead of faking confidence, embodying the luxury buyer's lifestyle inspires genuine confidence. You know your clients, you understand their world, and you can deliver the experience they desire. This confidence translates into every interaction, making luxury clients feel secure in choosing you. It also allows you to charge premium prices because your competence and confidence are undeniable. You'll grow into a more confident version of yourself because you've embodied the world in which you now exist.

HOW TO EMBODY THE LUXURY BUYER'S LIFESTYLE WITHOUT COMING FROM THAT WORLD

FOR THOSE WHO DIDN'T GROW up in a world of affluence, the idea of embodying a luxury lifestyle may seem daunting. I've had many attendees at speaking engagements express their fears and insecurities about serving such a high-end clientele. But it's not about becoming someone you're not. It's about deepening your understanding of what matters most to these clients and reflecting that in your relationship with them. Here are some ways to do that:

- **Research and Study the Luxury Market**
  Dive deep into the habits, preferences, and values of affluent buyers. This can be done through reading books, following luxury brands, and observing how high-end services operate as well as reading the magazines and blogs they read.

- **Immerse Yourself in the Luxury Experience**
  Visit high-end stores, experience fine dining, immerse yourself in high-end shopping districts, splurge on some luxurious services, and observe how luxury brands engage with their clientele. Pay attention to how they create a chic and personalized experience so you can literally see, hear, and feel what the luxury buyer is accustomed to experiencing.

- **Refine Your Brand**

    Ensure that every touchpoint of your brand, from your website to your in-person interactions, exudes sophistication, attention to detail, and excellence. My book, *LINGO,* is about learning to speak the secret language of your ideal customers and expressing it through brand messaging that resonates with luxury buyers. They need to know that you "get them" and speaking their lingo from marketing to delivery of services and beyond requires true embodiment.

◆ IN THE END...

TRULY EMBODYING THE LIFESTYLE OF luxury buyers is far more effective than "faking it" or relying on avatars and ideal client profiles. When you can genuinely step into their world, whether or not you come from it, you'll find that luxury buyers are more than willing to believe in who you are and invest in what you offer.

DIOR
The Importance of a Founder's Story

CHRISTIAN DIOR'S FOUNDING STORY IS a powerful reminder of the lasting impact of a visionary. In 1947, the designer launched The House of Dior with a mission to revive beauty and elegance in a post-war world. His debut collection introduced the revolutionary New Look—cinched waists, full skirts, and unapologetic glamour—offering hope and redefining women's fashion globally. As he walked to his first meeting with the future investor in the House of Dior, the designer found a "lucky star" lying on the ground along the Seine.

Though Dior led his brand for only a decade before his untimely passing in 1957 at just fifty-two, his influence endures as the cornerstone of the House of Dior. His vision and founder's story became the brand's DNA, including the lucky star, which to this day remains in the brand's iconic packaging.

Dior's successors, from Yves Saint Laurent to Maria Grazia Chiuri, have built on this foundation, honoring his principles while evolving with the times. Signature elements like the Bar Jacket and his love of floral motifs continually connect new collections to the brand's history.

Dior's journey illustrates the enduring importance of a founder's story: how it shapes a brand's values, inspires clients, and adds depth to its narrative. Whether the founder of a brand or a sales associate, the legacy of a founder's story reminds us that a clear, purpose-driven origin story can resonate across generations and make a brand truly timeless.

AN ELEVATED MINDSET

From Passive Service to Guided Expertise

SERVING THE LUXURY BUYER OFTEN requires an entire paradigm shift regarding what we think excellent service is—especially when it comes to the luxury market. We tend to think of luxury buyers as self-assured, having strong opinions, and meticulous: people who know precisely what they want and demand nothing short of excellence.

While these characteristics may hold some truth, there's a deeper, often misunderstood aspect to serving high-end clients. One that requires a mindset shift from passive service, giving them what they asked for, to guiding them with your expertise and providing options they never considered. This is how to stand out as a service provider.

Whether you're a business owner or sales associate, a concierge or massage therapist, new to the clientele, or have been serving them for decades, making the mindset shift from passive service to guided expertise will build stronger, more trustworthy, and long-lasting relationships.

MOVING BEYOND SERVICE TO LEADERSHIP

ONE OF THE MOST COMMON misconceptions about working with affluent clients is that they demand excellent service solely by accommodating their wishes and following their instructions. The reality is luxury clients choose the best in the first place and rely on your expertise to guide them. Whether you're their trusted landscaper or their preferred sales associate at their favorite fashion house, they have done their research and think you are their top choice. Now they want you to lead. To not just give them what they want but what you believe is best for them.

Yes, they may be very self-assured in what they want and believe is best for them. However, if you feel otherwise or have other options that you believe are better, you must present them.

This is a level of leadership many service providers haven't considered if their focus is on being accommodating. You certainly don't want to undermine their preferences but instead, enhance their experience and trust in you by applying your expertise in ways they may not have thought of. The true value comes when you introduce them to possibilities they didn't know existed and offer guidance that transforms ordinary service into exceptional service.

BE AN AUTHORITY WITH CONFIDENCE AND FINESSE

LUXURY CLIENTS APPRECIATE CONFIDENCE, ESPECIALLY from those they hire. They are accustomed to successful people and tend to value people who project authority. This is a key distinction in the luxury world. Rather than simply fulfilling requests, service providers in the luxury market should interact with their clients with a sense of authority. They should anticipate needs, identify opportunities, and, when appropriate, gently challenge clients' initial expectations with recommendations that are better suited for them.

It also takes some finesse to make sure your customers feel heard and yet offer better options at the same time. You need to take the time to delve deeper, ask better questions, consider what they are saying and what they are not saying, and gently suggest alternatives that elevate the outcome beyond what the client might have imagined. In other words, listen attentively yet stand by what you believe is best for them and let your luxury clients know that they're in good hands.

THE ROLE OF TRUST

In the luxury market, trust is paramount. An expert who is willing to say, "I understand what you're envisioning, but based on my experience, I'd recommend we consider this approach," or "this product instead," is far more likely to establish a long-lasting relationship with luxury clients than someone who passively follows directions.

What makes affluent clients so receptive to guided expertise is they are, at their core, people who understand the power of expertise and trust. They respect and respond to knowledgeable experts, and they appreciate service providers who step up and voice their opinions. Your viewpoint signals that the provider isn't simply delivering a transaction and giving them what they want, but is invested in their best interest and delivering the highest standard. This positions you as a partner and a trusted advisor rather than simply fulfilling their request. I sometimes joke that I do this so well that clients often ask me for suggestions for other types of services that have nothing to do with my own work. Of course, I'm happy to accommodate!

HELPFUL TIPS

For many service providers, making this shift requires both a new mindset and a rethinking of what service actually means. So here are a few helpful tips:

1. **Be Confident in Your Expertise:** Believe that your knowledge and experience add tremendous value to your client, whether it's a longstanding relationship or a quick retail exchange. Embrace your role as an expert and know that your insights are what separate you from everyone else.

2. **Active Listening:** Start with a deep understanding of the client's preferences and motivations. Ask questions that uncover deeper desires and goals that go beyond surface-level requests. Then you can offer suggestions with finesse.

3. **Offering Solutions, Not Just Options:** Luxury clients often prefer decisive, clear solutions over a list of options. Be careful not to overwhelm with too many options. Use your expertise to make specific recommendations that align with their intentions while elevating the outcome.

4. **Leading with Empathy and Grace:** Luxury service should never feel pushy or impersonal. Your suggestions should come from a place of genuine interest in the client's satisfaction, which makes your guidance feel thoughtful and truly in their best interest.

5. **Focusing on Relationship-Building:** Each interaction should be viewed as an opportunity to build trust and rapport. The more a client trusts your expertise, the more they'll value your guidance.

♦ IN THE END...

THE LUXURY MARKET REQUIRES A different level of service: one that combines attentive listening with a willingness to lead. By shifting from passive service to guided expertise, you can create experiences that resonate deeply with affluent clients, confirming your position as a trusted resource in addition to being a service provider. When service is also leadership, luxury clients don't just get what they want, they get what's best for them—and they value that.

DEALING WITH DISCOURAGEMENT

Building a Luxury Business Takes Time

BUILDING A LUXURY BUSINESS IS not the fastest route to building a successful business. It's a long game that requires patience, resilience, and steadfast commitment to your objectives. There will always be opportunities to make a quick dollar, take on less-than-ideal clients, and compromise your vision. But remember: anything high-end, whether a brand, a service, or a sales associate career, is not built overnight. Compromising along the way might feel like progress at the moment, but it can be nearly impossible to recover from in the long run.

Let's explore how to navigate the inevitable feelings of discouragement that arise on this slower, yet ultimately more rewarding, road to success.

YOU ARE NOT ALONE

WHEN DISCOURAGEMENT CREEPS IN, THE first thing to remember is this—**you are not alone.** Every business owner, entrepreneur, and sales associate with similar luxury market aspirations experiences these moments, no matter what they claim or what their social media feed looks like. Social media tends to show only the highlights, even more so in the luxury space where looking posh and polished is the objective. Don't let appearances fool you. Remember that comparison is the thief of joy. In what can be an appearance-driven culture of luxury, know that everyone is walking the same uphill battle to the pinnacle of the high-end and faces discouragement at some point. You are in good company.

DISCOURAGEMENT OFTEN PRECEDES BREAKTHROUGHS

ONE OF THE MOST IMPORTANT lessons I've learned is that discouragement often strikes just before a breakthrough. It may sound trite but there's just too much evidence that it's true to discard it. It's as though your inner exhaustion from putting in the work amplifies those feelings.

A few years ago, I hit a plateau in my business and confided in my friend, Dorie Clark, author of *The Long Game*. When I shared my frustration, her response was simple: "You're smart; you'll figure it out."

At the time, I found that advice frustrating. It felt too simplistic. I thought to myself, "Really? Is that all you've got?" But she wasn't wrong. I did figure it out, and in hindsight, I appreciated that she saw my potential when I couldn't see it myself.

If you're feeling discouraged, remind yourself that others often recognize your progress better than you can. Trust their perspective and believe that you are closer to your goals than you think.

REALITY CHECK: HOW FAR OFF ARE YOU?

DISCOURAGEMENT HAS A WAY OF distorting reality, making the gap between where you are and where you want to be feel larger than it is. When those feelings arise, take a moment to do a reality check.

Ask yourself:

- How far am I, really, from my goal?
- Is the gap manageable?
- Is the progress I've made so far a sign that my goal is achievable?

More often than not, you'll find that you're closer than you think. By stepping back and assessing your situation objectively, whether through financial numbers, milestones, or personal growth, you can diffuse the over-dramatization that discouragement feeds on.

EVERY EFFORT IS A SWING AT BAT

HIGH-END BUSINESSES AREN'T BUILT ON luck. They're built on consistent effort, persistence, and the willingness to take swing after swing, even when you miss.

I once interviewed Antuan Raimone, a Broadway performer from *Hamilton*, about the rejection he's faced in his career as a lifelong Broadway performer. He told me he journals about every audition he's ever done. While most of those auditions didn't lead to roles, journaling served as a reminder of how much effort he had put in.

Your journey is no different. Every effort—every pitch, proposal, client meeting, or project—is a swing at bat. Each one brings you closer to success, even if the immediate result is a miss. Instead of seeing effort as a measure of failure, reframe it as proof of how close you are to achieving your goals. Because success in the luxury market is never fast, consistent effort is key.

WHY THE LONG ROAD IS WORTH IT

HIGH-END BUSINESSES AREN'T BUILT FOR speed. They're built for endurance. The luxury market thrives on reputation, trust, and a deep understanding of what your clients value. These are not things that can be rushed or compromised.

Think about Home Depot. It's a great brand for what it does, but it could never become a high-end boutique. Why? Because it's built on entirely different principles. Similarly, if you compromise your objectives to chase quick wins, you risk undermining your ability to serve the luxury market in the long term. Don't compromise your values. Don't undermine your vision. Don't dilute your brand. It may be slower, but in the long run, so very worth it.

HOW TO STAY ENCOURAGED ON THE LONG ROAD

1. **Celebrate Your Effort, Not Just the Outcome**

    Discouragement often stems from focusing too much on outcomes and not enough on effort. Acknowledge every swing at bat, even the misses, as proof of your persistence.

2. **Surround Yourself with Encouragement**

    Whether it's through mentors, friends, or colleagues, seek out people who see your progress even when you can't. Their perspective can provide the boost you need to keep going.

3. **Immerse Yourself in the World You're Building**

    Spend time experiencing the luxury market firsthand. Visit high-end boutiques, dine at fine restaurants, or simply observe the level of service and attention to detail in these spaces. These experiences can reignite your passion and remind you why the long road is worth it.

◆ IN THE END...

THE KEY IS TO STAY. The luxury market rewards those who stay in the game. Yes, it takes time. Yes, it's harder to stay committed when the road feels endless. But you've already put in the effort. You've set the stage for success. Now, the key is to stay the course.

Stay committed to your vision. Stay patient with the process. Stay focused on the fact that you're closer than you think. This isn't just about building a business—it's about building a dream. And the long road, while challenging, is the one that will take you there.

BELONGING

Finding Your Place in the World of Luxury Service

FOR MANY LUXURY BUSINESS OWNERS and sales associates, the journey into serving the affluent can feel like stepping into an unfamiliar world. The sprawling estates, designer wardrobes, conversations about private jets or exotic vacations and the money they spend, even at your own place of business, can create an uncomfortableness and distance between realities. It's easy to feel like an outsider, constantly second-guessing your every move, word, or gesture. But here's the truth—belonging isn't about the exterior world. It's about what's within you.

I've often said that, in many ways, I felt more comfortable in the massive homes of my ultra-wealthy clients than I did in my own childhood home. It wasn't about the material wealth surrounding me. It was about a deeper connection to shared values, lifestyle, and a sense of mutual respect. While my family and where I grew up was obviously familiar to me, I can't say I felt like I belonged. I found that feeling when I discovered "my people"—those I was meant to serve.

It's my heartfelt desire that opening up this conversation about belonging will help luxury business owners and sales associates not just get past any possible uncertainties and insecurities they may have, but truly develop a sense of belonging regardless of where they come from and where they end up. It is then that belonging becomes fertile ground for thriving.

THE ILLUSION OF "FITTING IN"

WHEN WE FEEL LIKE OUTSIDERS, our first instinct is often to try to "fit in." We may try to be in the know, memorize wine lists, or drop designer names into conversations, hoping to camouflage ourselves into the environment. But fitting in is not the same as belonging. Fitting in is performative. It requires you to mold yourself to someone else's expectations. Belonging, on the other hand, is an internal state of being—it comes from knowing who you are and what value you bring to the table.

The affluent clients you serve are perceptive. They can sense authenticity just as quickly as they can sense insecurity. They aren't necessarily looking for you to be like them or live up to their stature. They're looking for someone who can make them feel seen, understood, and taken care of. That doesn't require you to have a yacht or a villa in Tuscany—it requires confidence in yourself and your abilities.

BELONGING COMES FROM WITHIN

BELONGING ISN'T SOMETHING SOMEONE ELSE can grant you; it's something you must claim for yourself. It's a choice to show up fully, as you are, and trust that who you are is enough. In luxury service, your expertise, attention to detail, and ability to anticipate needs are your greatest assets, not your wardrobe or your background.

When I first started working with affluent clients, I felt a sense of awe and intimidation. But I realized something important. These clients weren't judging me based on where I came from. I don't think they even gave it a thought. They were evaluating the quality of the experience I provided. The more I leaned into what I did well, the more confident I became, and the less I worried about fitting in.

FINDING YOUR PEOPLE

ONE OF THE MOST POWERFUL realizations you can have is that belonging isn't universal—it's specific. You don't need to belong everywhere, you just need to belong somewhere. For luxury service providers, that somewhere is often with the clients you feel most aligned with and who value what you bring to their lives.

When you find clients who appreciate your approach, your care, and your expertise, something shifts. The invisible wall disappears. Conversations become easier, interactions feel natural, and you realize that the sense of otherness was never about them. It was about your own inner talk.

BELONGING IS A CHOICE

AT THE END OF THE day, belonging isn't about whether you grew up in a wealthy family, attended the right schools, or have the right social connections. It's about whether you can stand in your space with confidence, knowing that you have every right to be there because of the value you bring.

When you stop worrying about fitting in and start focusing on showing up authentically, something magical happens. You'll realize that you do belong. Not because someone else says you do, but because you've claimed that space for yourself.

KEEP IN MIND:

1. **Own Your Expertise:** Your knowledge, skills, and ability to serve at a high level are your ticket to belonging. Focus on what you excel at and let that confidence shine through.
2. **Focus on Service, Not Status:** Your role isn't to match your clients' lifestyles—it's to enhance them. Keep your focus on how you can serve, and the connection will follow.
3. **Stay Curious:** Ask genuine questions, show interest in your clients' preferences, and let go of the need to know it all. Curiosity builds connection.

4. **Redefine Success:** Success in luxury service isn't about being accepted into an elite club—it's about creating meaningful moments and building trust.
5. **Surround Yourself with Support:** Connect with peers who understand your journey. Whether it's a mentor, a coach, or a community, having support reinforces your sense of belonging.

◆ IN THE END...

WHEN YOU OPERATE FROM A place of belonging, your interactions change. You're no longer holding back, overthinking, or hesitating. You're fully present, fully engaged, and fully capable of delivering an exceptional experience. And that is what clients, regardless of their wealth or status, are truly looking for.

Belonging isn't about them. It's about you. It's about recognizing your worth, claiming your space, and stepping confidently into the world you were meant to serve. Because when you belong to yourself, you can belong anywhere.

ELEMENT III

Luxury Buyer Behavior

It's easy to assume that luxury buyers are driven purely by status or the desire for perfection, but this oversimplification fails to capture the layered motivations behind their behaviors.

LUXURY BUYER BEHAVIOR
Introduction

THE FOLLOWING ELEMENT ON LUXURY Buyer Behavior is by far the largest, and for good reason. Nothing will ever be more important than understanding what makes your clients "tick." I like to use the word "tick" because it suggests a commitment to truly knowing a person's mindset, behavior, responses, perspective, and emotions. This requires that you appreciate and respect the whole of what drives someone, not just their actions, but the internal factors that shape those behaviors. I believe it's far more respectful and compassionate to consider the entirety of a person rather than attribute any single behavior to one characteristic. This approach is especially critical when working with luxury clients who are sophisticated, varied, and—without this holistic comprehension—could be challenging to serve.

By opening our minds and hearts to serve with empathy and understanding, we can better appreciate why the behavior and mindset of affluent people may be more complex and nuanced than most.

For one, affluence often comes with a layered and intricate background story. For those born into wealth, there can be generations of family dynamics, legacies, and expectations that shape who they are and how they behave. For the self-made affluent, the story is different but no less rich with complexity. Self-made individuals often carry a story of resilience and tenacity, of navigating obstacles and taking risks, and countless turning points that helped shape their view of success.

One of the things that stood out to me when working intimately with wealthy clients over multiple decades is that I could never quite tell who came from inherited wealth and who was self-made. This wasn't because I hadn't come to know them well, but rather because wealth itself becomes a kind of equalizer of certain behavioral patterns. There's a common ground that forms—a subtle shared outlook on life and decision-making that's bigger than the origin of their wealth. This is not to say their stories are identical, but rather that it seems wealth itself tends to shape certain conduct, creating a layer of shared behaviors among the affluent that are as subtle as they are complex. This is why understanding luxury buyer behavior is paramount and the reason this is the largest of all Elements.

These differentiating behaviors when it comes to financial decisions include being emotionally driven, adapting to and embracing market changes quickly, setting trends in discretionary purchases, having their identity enmeshed in brands and purchases, and investing substantially in relationships.

Another aspect of luxury buyer behavior is its paradoxical nature. At first glance, it might seem like luxury buyers want to be treated with formality at all times. While they do value professionalism and high standards, there's also a place and time for casualness. In fact, many of them deeply appreciate service professionals who can be both competent and straightforward, bringing a sense of ease and sincerity to their interactions. They may appear to demand the utmost in quality and perfection yet can be completely understanding when something goes wrong if it's handled with genuine care and respect. They may relish luxury brands and elite products yet feel equally at home in a well-worn pair of jeans or a comfortable sweater. This isn't a contradiction as much as an understanding of the balanced and nuanced lives of many luxury buyers—and human nature!

Wealthy clients also demonstrate paradoxes in their relationships. They may keep a carefully chosen inner circle, selecting friends and associates with intention and discernment. And yet, it's not uncommon for them to form lasting friendships with service providers, people they interact with regularly who offer warmth, sincerity, and a lack of pretense. There's something refreshing and grounding about these relationships that luxury clients often cherish. The luxury buyer is far from monolithic, and as their service provider, it's essential not to expect them to be predictable. Attempting to figure them out in rigid terms will only limit your ability to connect and serve effectively, especially in a respectful, individual manner.

Perhaps the best way to describe the behavior and psychology of luxury buyers is nuanced. Their mindset is complex and subtle, much like a fine wine, an exquisitely designed home, or a carefully curated gallery art show. Each choice and preference has layers, sometimes clear, sometimes hidden, and those who choose to step into the arena of serving the affluent should expect the journey to be both complex and beautiful. One of the biggest mistakes I see service providers make is entering the luxury market with preconceived notions or judgments about affluent clients. It's easy to assume that luxury buyers are driven purely by status or the desire for perfection, but this oversimplification fails to capture the layered motivations behind their behaviors. When providers approach each client as an individual, free from assumptions, they gain a far richer understanding of what drives luxury clients and, in turn, deliver a more personalized and impactful service. They may also be surprised to create a far richer experience for themselves, as well.

Given the nuanced mindset and behavior of luxury clients, it's essential for luxury service providers to refine their listening and observational skills. Listening, in this context, isn't just about hearing the words spoken. It's about picking up on subtleties, reading between the lines, understanding unspoken preferences, and recognizing the small details that reveal a client's true desires and values.

This is why I often say, "I don't just know this market, I was in their closets," having been their family portrait photographer. Yes, often literally in the closet while helping them prepare for a session. But more importantly, also metaphorically, as these are the intimate conversations and observations that develop the strongest bonds. This is where empathy becomes indispensable. Luxury clients want to feel deeply seen and understood, to sense that their needs and expectations are known on a level beyond the transactional. This kind of connection requires a provider to be fully present, attentive, and responsive to the client's individual ways of being, communicating, and experiencing the world.

In an industry that increasingly relies on data and market research, it's easy to assume that numbers alone can define and predict client behavior. But ultimately, no amount of data, research, or trend analysis will ever be as valuable as a thorough understanding of what makes a luxury buyer tick. Their motivations are complex, often influenced by personal experiences, evolving tastes, and personal values that can shift over time. The key is to understand the broader mindset and behavior of the affluent clientele while treating each client as a unique individual, open to the nuanced influences that shape their values and choices. Providers who make the effort to truly understand their clients, who go beyond assumptions and remain open to the subtle complexities at play, are better equipped to create meaningful, memorable experiences that leave a lasting impact.

Effectively serving luxury buyers means stepping into their world, gaining their trust, appreciating the values that guide their decisions, and respecting the behaviors that drive them. This requires empathy, patience, and a willingness to continually learn and adapt. While the luxury market may present its challenges, for those who are dedicated to understanding affluent clients, it offers unparalleled opportunities for connection, lasting success, and personal growth.

DECODING DIVERSE BUYERS

The Loyalist and the Aspirational

WHEN IT COMES TO LUXURY brands and service providers, customer loyalty has always been the crown jewel. The loyal luxury buyer isn't just a customer, they're a raving fan. Their identity is intertwined with the brands they love and the service providers they trust. This relationship goes far beyond transactions. It's built on shared values, impeccable service, and unmatched quality.

But while loyal customers have long been the cornerstone of luxury businesses, there's a new player in the luxury market—the aspirational buyer. These two groups bring different expectations, behaviors, and opportunities for your business. Understanding and catering to both is critical if you want to thrive in today's diverse luxury landscape.

THE LOYALIST

LOYAL LUXURY BUYERS ARE THE dream clients. They keep coming back, year after year, because they see your brand or service as part of their identity. These aren't casual customers—they're deeply invested in the relationship they've built with you and feel a kinship with the brand.

Why does this matter so much? Because loyalty translates into long customer lifecycles and consistent revenue. More importantly, loyalists require less effort to keep than it takes to win new customers. They know your value, trust your brand, and expect you to deliver on it every time.

I always encourage businesses to review their customer loyalty rate annually. A drop in loyalty is often the first sign of a bigger problem. It could signal declining service quality, changes in your product, or even a shift in how business growth has affected client relationships. This is an all too common problem. Growth, while exciting, can alienate early adopters and make those loyal customers feel overlooked as your business scales. It's essential to strike a balance. Growth shouldn't come at the expense of the people who helped you get there and a drop in customer loyalty rate is the first warning of a bigger problem to be solved.

The loyalist's devotion is hard-won and easily lost. If they feel they're no longer getting the same level of care or attention, their disappointment can cause them to leave. And let's face it, earning back a loyalist's trust is far harder than earning it the first time.

WINNING OVER THE LOYALIST

FOR LOYAL BUYERS, IT'S ALL about consistency, trust, and familiarity. They want to feel like VIPs at every touchpoint. That means personalized service, attention to detail, and reinforcing the relationship they've built with you.

Loyalists value discretion and reliability. Their loyalty stems from knowing you'll deliver every time, without question.

THE ASPIRATIONAL

ENTER THE ASPIRATIONAL BUYER. THESE customers may not have the same consistent purchasing power as loyalists, but they bring something equally valuable—enthusiasm and visibility.

Aspirational buyers are typically experiencing luxury as a treat, perhaps for the first time. For them, buying a luxury product or service isn't just a transaction, it's a milestone. They're driven by the excitement of the experience and the desire to share it with others.

This group offers a unique opportunity. While their purchases may be less frequent or even one-time, aspirational buyers are your loudest advocates. They'll share their experience with friends, and all over on social media, likely with a selfie or three, with a level of enthusiasm that loyal buyers often don't.

In fact, the aspirational buyer's excitement can drive brand awareness in ways your loyalist base might not. Loyal customers often value discretion; they don't need to tell the world where they shop or who they hire. Aspirational buyers, on the other hand, are more likely to shout it from the rooftops.

And don't underestimate the long-term potential here. Today's aspirational buyer could very well become tomorrow's loyalist. As you'll read below, I've lived this firsthand.

DAZZLING THE ASPIRATIONAL BUYER

FOR ASPIRATIONAL BUYERS, IT'S ABOUT creating unforgettable moments. They want experiences that feel classy and extraordinary. Even if their interaction with your brand is brief, it should leave a lasting impression.

These buyers thrive on novelty and storytelling. They're more likely to post on social media about their experience or tell their friends about the incredible service they received. Think of this group as your built-in brand ambassadors, even if their purchases are smaller and less often.

BALANCING BOTH

SERVING BOTH LOYALISTS AND ASPIRATIONAL buyers requires tailored strategies. What resonates with one group won't necessarily captivate the other.

FROM ASPIRATIONAL TO LOYAL: MY STORY

YEARS AGO, AS A STRUGGLING photographer trying to make a name for myself, I loved visiting Bergdorf Goodman on Fifth Avenue in New York City. It was an aspirational experience for me. I couldn't afford much, but I'd ask for small items—like $20 gifts—to be gift wrapped just for the experience.

What stood out was how I was treated. The staff never made me feel like I didn't belong. Their graciousness and professionalism stayed with me. As my career grew, so did my ability to invest in the brands I once aspired to be part of. Today, I'm a loyal customer of Bergdorf Goodman—a transformation from aspirational buyer to devoted customer. I mention this not to brag. But rather for me, it's the best representation that what I teach works. Second, this is the power of treating every customer, no matter their purchasing power at that moment, with respect and care. You never know what aspirational customer might become your next loyalist.

◆ IN THE END...

THE WORLD OF LUXURY IS no longer one-dimensional. To succeed, you need to embrace both the steadfast loyalty of your regulars and the enthusiasm of your aspirational buyers.

Ignoring one group in favor of the other is a missed opportunity. Loyalists bring stability, while aspirational buyers bring reach and future potential. Together, they form a diverse ecosystem that can drive a luxury business forward in ways you might not expect. It's a tapestry of long-standing relationships and one-time moments, each valuable in its own way.

Whether you're catering to a loyalist or an aspirational buyer, the key is to check assumptions at the door. Treat every customer interaction as an opportunity to create something meaningful. Snobbery as a means to come across as "exclusive" need not exist.

By understanding these two types of luxury buyers and being sure you are speaking to each, you'll not only expand your reach but also deepen your impact. And that's what true luxury is all about—crafting experiences that leave a lasting impression.

LUXURY BUYERS

The First Responders of Change

WHEN THE WORLD CHANGES, LUXURY buyers are the first to react. They're quick to adapt, adjust, and pivot, sometimes dramatically when the tides of the economy, culture, or society change. In my experience, this behavior surprises people, but it's important to note: this a defining trait of the luxury market.

Luxury buyers are emotionally driven, deeply attuned to the world around them, and often unafraid to embrace change. Whether it's in response to economic downturns, social upheaval, a global crisis like 9/11, the Great Recession, or the COVID-19 pandemic, you can expect your luxury buyers to react first.

As we look at the reasons luxury buyers are often the first to respond to change, here's also a precautionary tale. It's one thing to grasp the buyer behavior, but quite another to prepare yourself for the after-effects. It's what I refer to as The Period Post-Crisis and it's the period of time two to three years after what appears to be the beginning of recovery.

Once the world gets on the other side of a significant event, there's a period of recovery, enthusiasm, and gratefulness for having made it through. But then, two to three years later, the effect the change had on people's lives starts to show up. How values changed and what buyers find most important may now be misaligned with prior marketing messages. Some businesses and individuals recover very well. Others, not so well. Those businesses that have not recovered as well might look at those that have and wonder what they are doing wrong. Then, of course, the mental toll and stress of change can often take some time to show up. Heed this as a precaution to be prepared for The Period

Post-Crisis and also as a reminder to be graceful with yourself after a time of significant change.

The faster rate at which luxury buyers respond to these circumstances can exasperate the resources of the luxury service provider. Let's explore why luxury buyers are often the "first responders" of consumer behavior, how their quick reactions influence the market, and what businesses can learn from their ever-changing nature.

WHY LUXURY BUYERS REACT FIRST

LUXURY BUYERS AREN'T JUST TREND followers, they're trendsetters. They're often at the forefront of social and economic shifts for a couple of key reasons:

- **Emotional Decision-Making:** Luxury purchases by definition are rarely about necessity. Instead, they're driven by emotions— how something feels, what it symbolizes, or how it aligns with a buyer's personal values or current experience. This deeply-felt connection to the purchase makes working with luxury buyers a bit of an emotional rollercoaster.

- **Financial Flexibility:** Unlike the average consumer, luxury buyers have the resources to pivot quickly. They can afford to shift their spending habits faster than most. They will stop spending or start spending as they see fit based on in-the-moment information as well as future predictions. I periodically had clients halt an order just placed because the market crashed the day after and then call back a short time later to get it going again because the market picked up. I assure you, their entire financial stability was not on the line because of their portrait order but sometimes they acted as if it was.

- **Luxury buyers also** often behave the opposite of the general populous. For example, when they have concerns for the future economy, they use credit less and pay more often with cash. They typically use credit cards for the benefits, not because the money isn't available. But in the interest of more careful management during unpredictable times, the benefits don't outweigh the desire for careful financial management. Almost every other sector of society goes more in debt with credit cards during challenging times.

This responsiveness means businesses catering to the luxury market must stay on their toes. Understanding the emotional pulse of luxury buyers is key to staying relevant in a rapidly changing world.

TRENDS THAT SHIFT IN LUXURY

ONE OF THE MOST FASCINATING aspects of luxury buyers is how quickly their preferences evolve. Here are some of the most notable ways I have witnessed their behavior shifts:

- **From Exclusivity to Accessibility**
  Luxury buyers crave exclusivity, until they don't. The moment something becomes too mainstream, it often loses its appeal. This is what I call the "class-to-mass" shift. Once everyone is in the know, the allure fades.

  For businesses, this is a delicate balance. You want your brand to be desirable and recognized, but not so popular that it feels overexposed. Staying "in" while maintaining a sense of exclusivity requires constant innovation and brand consideration. I witnessed this first hand as the popularity of the custom holiday cards I created for my clients grew in popularity. What started out as a few thousand cards a year grew to nearly 20,000 cards a year, all adorned by portraits by the same photographer. Clients started expressing concern their cards might look like someone else's. To this clientele, that would be like two women showing up at a gala wearing the same dress. I made it my point to know who knew who, whose kids went to the same private schools, what communities in The Hamptons they had summer homes, all so I could be sure no two holiday cards looked alike if there was any chance of overlap. I let my clients know of this effort and assured them that my photography style, while recognizable, was also creative and that since they were a unique family, that no two custom-designed holiday cards would ever look alike.

It's worth also pointing out here that producing holidays cards was far from the most profitable side of my photography business yet, as you can see, received a tremendous amount of attention. It was this dedication and attention to what I'm sure my clients knew was not the mainstay of my business that let them know that I cared more about what was important to them than what was important to me. Think for a moment about the signal that sends to your luxury buyers.

- **Self-Expression Takes Center Stage**

     Luxury buyers use their purchases to express who they are and what they value. What's fascinating is how quickly this self-expression changes.

     One day, it's all about minimalism—clean lines, neutral tones, and understated elegance. The next, it's bold, extravagant, and making a statement. One moment it's about showing off every logo, the next it's about quiet luxury. It's less about the product itself and more about how it reflects their mood or identity in the moment.

- **The Luxury of Time**

  The interconnectedness between luxury and time has shifted dramatically. There was a time when the value of a luxury experience was measured by how much time it consumed. Today, saving time is often the luxury itself.

  Luxury buyers now fall into two camps: those who want in-depth, immersive experiences and those who value efficiency and time savings. Businesses must be prepared to accommodate both.

BALANCING CHANGE WITH TRADITION

WITH ALL THIS CONSTANT EVOLUTION, you might wonder if there's room for tradition in the world of luxury. The answer is yes, but only if it's paired with innovation.

Craftsmanship, legacy, and timeless elegance will always have a place in luxury. Buyers appreciate brands with a strong sense of history, as long as they also remain relevant. Every luxury brand runs the risk of feeling outdated at some point. Or too mainstream. The most successful luxury brands strike a delicate balance: they innovate to stay current while maintaining the integrity of their legacy. It's about being fresh enough to capture attention and enduring enough to hold it.

TIPS

1. **Stay Agile:** Change is constant, and luxury buyers expect businesses to keep up. This means being ready to pivot quickly in response to societal shifts or emerging trends.
2. **Be Emotionally Intelligent:** Luxury buyers make decisions based on how something makes them feel. Tapping into those emotions is far more effective than focusing solely on features or benefits.

3. **Balance Innovation with Tradition:** Don't abandon your roots, but don't let them hold you back either. Luxury buyers value both heritage and forward-thinking ideas.

◆ IN THE END...

THE WORLD IS EVOLVING FASTER than ever, and luxury buyers are leading the way. Their quick reactions, emotional depth, and trendsetting nature make them a fascinating and challenging audience to serve.

But within this challenge lies an incredible opportunity. By staying attuned to the ever-changing behaviors of luxury buyers, businesses can remain relevant, innovative, and exceptional.

So here's to the luxury buyers: the first responders of change. They keep us on our toes, push us to evolve, and remind us that in the world of luxury, the only constant is transformation.

BROWN JORDAN
Intentionally Subtle Branding

AS A PHOTOGRAPHER, I SPENT a great deal of time rearranging outdoor furniture to create the optimal setting. One thing that was abundantly clear in the world of luxury outdoor furniture was that Brown Jordan was the brand of choice.

Two features uniquely position Brown Jordan as the go-to for affluent buyers: its subtle branding and its alignment with a sophisticated outdoor lifestyle.

Brown Jordan's understated branding is a hallmark of its appeal. In a market where many luxury products flaunt their logos, Brown Jordan opts for discretion. Its pieces are designed to let their quality and craftsmanship speak for themselves, without overt branding. For luxury buyers, this approach is not just a preference but a statement. It aligns with their desire for quality and sophistication without the need for showiness. Brown Jordan's restraint resonates deeply with customers who prefer their outdoor spaces to have an air of elegant leisure.

Equally significant is the brand's understanding of its customer's leisure lifestyle. Brown Jordan doesn't just sell furniture; it offers an aspirational vision of outdoor living. The brand's marketing emphasizes moments of relaxation, gatherings with loved ones, and a seamless blend of comfort and sophistication. For affluent buyers, these are not mere promises—they are reflections of their reality and aspirations. Brown Jordan's ability to evoke these ideals transforms its furniture into more than products. They become the basis for creating meaningful, luxurious experiences—and family portraits.

BREAKING THROUGH THE ORDINARY

Going Beyond Quality, Exclusivity, and Price

THE TYPICAL IMAGE OF THE luxury buyer has evolved considerably in recent years, shifting from an older, wealthy individual to a variety of people of different ages and ethnicities who are driven by various motivations. Whether it's Millennials, Gen Z, or the ultra-affluent, today's luxury buyers are not just looking for material possessions. They are seeking self-expression, meaning, and experiences.

Therefore, the conversation needs to change. Many luxury brands and businesses continue to focus on three key selling points that may not matter as much as in previous decades: quality, exclusivity, and price. While these factors are certainly important, they may no longer hold the same weight they once did. Today's luxury buyers expect these things as a baseline; they're non-negotiable. To truly stand out, luxury brands must break through these ordinary conversations and tap into deeper, more meaningful connections and experiences with their clientele.

In this context, conversations about quality, exclusivity, and price alone are becoming passé. These attributes are expected in the luxury market, but they're no longer enough to create distinction. Buyers know they're paying for high-quality products and exclusivity when they opt for luxury goods, but that's not what captivates them. Luxury brands must now appeal to a more complex set of desires and values, attracting luxury buyers in much more emotional, intimate, and personalized ways.

MOVING BEYOND QUALITY

FIRST, LET'S TAKE A LOOK at the conversations around quality. In the past, the assumption has been that quality is the strongest selling point when appealing to luxury buyers, but that's only true up to a point. Luxury buyers already expect a high level of craftsmanship and quality when paying for luxury goods and services. Reinforcing these features in marketing won't differentiate a brand from its competitors.

To stand out, luxury brands need to elevate the conversation. Instead of simply highlighting quality, for example, brands can emphasize the story behind the creation of a product and the underlying benefits of luxury services. For many buyers, particularly the younger generations, the values a brand represents and its mission matter. The story about how a brand betters the world while maintaining high quality is captivating. It's no longer just about owning something of high quality. It's about owning something of quality that also tells a story and reflects their values.

IS EXCLUSIVITY WHAT THEY REALLY WANT?

IT NEVER CEASES TO AMAZE me how often exclusivity is promoted with luxury brands and in luxury marketing without much thought about how its focus may be coming across. It's become a rote way of speaking about luxury to the point where today it may have lost its impact or is creating the wrong impression. Let's not simply slap exclusive on it in the name of luxury, but rather challenge ourselves to consider what it is we're really trying to say and what it means to the customer. Furthermore, and most importantly, not used properly, exclusivity can come across as tone-deaf. Exclusive as in special or limited edition is fine. Exclusive as in excluding people may come across very differently. Just imagine the implication of an "exclusive" country club. Yes, it could come across as high-end. It could also come across as code for "only certain people are welcome." What's the real intention of the message? Is it worth the risk?

However, challenging the notion of exclusivity in luxury poses one of the greatest challenges for luxury businesses and brands—maintaining a premier brand image without coming across as inappropriately exclusive of others.

The concept of exclusivity has been the cornerstone of luxury marketing. Haute couture, limited-edition collections, and experiences only available for a select group have been much of the appeal of luxury goods and services.

However, the mindset of today's luxury buyers is evolving, and the old exclusivity model no longer resonates with this demographic as it once did. That's not to say such goods and services are available to everyone. That defies the idea of luxury. But the misuse of marketing exclusivity may be out of touch with buyer psychology today, as the concept is increasingly also tied to the idea that other people are being excluded, and being less inclusive can become a moral challenge for many of today's luxury buyers.

Businesses and brands that can position themselves as exceptional, above the ordinary, while also coming across as inclusive, will win the affection of today's luxury buyers. In my forty years in business serving the ultra-luxury market, I have witnessed the necessary transformation of the word exclusive from being a primary marketing term to carefully used so as not to become a dirty word.

A very delicate balance indeed. How to make your luxury buyers feel special, their investment worth it, and recognize their privilege to afford such goods and services without causing them to question their values? Perhaps less focus on being exclusive and more focus on recognition and gratitude for one's good fortune.

PRICING TELLS A STORY

IN THE PAST, LUXURY GOODS and services were often synonymous with high price tags, with the assumption that expensive is automatically equated to luxury. However, in today's evolving market, simply pricing something high is no longer enough to make it feel truly luxurious.

For one, buyers expect more than calling it luxury just based on cost. They seek deeper meaning and personal connection in their purchases. A high price point without an accompanying story, experience, or unique value proposition often falls flat. In fact, a high price without context can even alienate potential buyers.

Additionally, today's consumers are savvy and well-informed. They can easily compare prices across brands and markets, making it difficult for any business to rely on price alone to create the perception of luxury. The true essence of luxury now lies in how a product or service aligns with personal values, offers a unique experience, or adds to their lifestyle.

To stand out in today's market, luxury brands need to move beyond pricing strategies and focus on delivering a holistic experience. Simply put, luxury today is less about the price and more about the meaning behind the purchase.

◆ IN THE END...

WHERE QUALITY, EXCLUSIVITY, AND PRICE are no longer enough to differentiate a brand, luxury companies must evolve their strategies to attract today's consumers. By moving beyond these traditional selling points, luxury brands can create lasting impressions that resonate with today's diverse and educated buyers.

The future of luxury lies in its ability to make customers feel special, not just because of their purchasing power, but because they are part of the larger narrative of the brand that speaks to their identity, values, and emotions. When luxury brands can do that, they will not only stand out but also thrive.

HOW TO ENSURE BUYERS FEEL CONFIDENT IN THEIR PURCHASES

LUXURY GOODS AND SERVICE PROVIDERS have an additional responsibility to their luxury buyers that often gets overlooked. It can be easy to assume that when money isn't an issue and the purchase is perhaps an easy one, that your customer doesn't also need to feel good about their purchase. Hardly anything can be further from the truth.

There is a delicate dance between indulgence and justification that many luxury buyers experience. No matter how easy the purchase is for the luxury buyer, they also want to feel good about their purchase and decision. There are many things a luxury business and brand can and should do to instill confidence, help their customers justify the expense, and all around feel great about their purchasing decision.

SHOW THE CRAFTSMANSHIP

ON A RECENT TRIP, I had an experience at one of the finest brands Paris has to offer: a visit to the iconic Dior store and La Galerie Dior at 30 Avenue Montaigne. First, there was the purchase, which of course was a wonderful experience. There were a couple of items I was in pursuit of. But it was after the purchase that the magic happened. That was a visit to La Galerie Dior, an extensive museum and history timeline of Christian Dior and the iconic House of Dior.

Once educated about the history of this iconic luxury brand, and exposed to the incredible details of the work, the unwavering craftsmanship, the brilliance of the design, and the depth of care for the Paris ladies he designed for, any purchase would be fully justified. Suddenly, the most expensive of purchases would feel like the value is greater than the investment.

In my photography business, I sourced and offered portrait frames that were hand carved and finished in 22kt gold. They were an investment and one that clients would often question. Once I provided a video of the process and craftsmanship, the questions were quelled and clients often commented they were surprised the frames didn't cost more.

Allow your luxury buyers to experience the craftsmanship, hard work, and attention to detail that goes into the goods and services you provide. Chances are that if you're as good as you likely are, you make it look easy. Show the background story, do your buyers a favor, and help them feel great about their buying decision.

UNDERSTAND THE EMOTIONAL CONNECTION

OFTEN LUXURY BUYERS HAVE A reason for their purchase that may not seem obvious. Inquire as to why this purchase is meaningful or important to them. Perhaps the purchase is to commemorate a special occasion or holds a deeper meaning. When purchasing a shirt at one of my favorite designers in Paris, the sales associate wisely asked if this was a gift. When I explained it was a birthday gift for myself, he quickly congratulated me and reached into a drawer to provide me with a card pre-signed for such occasions by the designer himself. Had he not asked, I would have missed this meaningful keepsake and the moment to enjoy the experience even more.

Luxury purchases often have meaning. Take the time to inquire about the emotional connection the buyer has to that purchasing decision and the experience now outweighs any concern there may have been about the investment.

VALUES AND TRANSPARENCY

By fostering a deeper understanding of the brand's culture and values, buyers can appreciate the intrinsic worth of their purchases beyond the price tag. Similarly, transparency is another key element in building buyer confidence. Luxury buyers are discerning individuals who seek authenticity and integrity in their purchases. Therefore, brands must be forthcoming about their sourcing, production processes, and ethical practices. Whether it's sustainable materials, fair labor practices, or charitable initiatives, highlighting these aspects not only aligns with the values of conscientious luxury consumers but also reinforces the notion that their luxury indulgence is contributing to a greater good.

POST-PURCHASE EXPERIENCE

Lastly, creating a post-purchase experience and reassurance is essential in ensuring buyer satisfaction. Luxury buyers expect impeccable service during the purchase transaction. It's not easy to impress there. But you can impress and provide reassurance in their decision with exceptional post-purchase experience. I have to say, I think luxury brands in Paris do this better than any place in the world. Whether it's a follow-up text, email, or a phone call checking in a day or so later, these are the personalized post-purchase experiences that go the extra mile to ensure customer satisfaction, demonstrate a commitment to excellence, and foster long-term loyalty. A simple check-in about how a client is feeling after an afternoon at the spa or asking about how a gift was received can be much appreciated gestures and give a buyer confidence they made the right decision.

◆ IN THE END...

MAKING LUXURY BUYERS FEEL BETTER about their purchases requires a multifaceted approach that goes beyond the product itself. By emphasizing craftsmanship, the emotional connection, values and transparency, and a post-purchase experience, luxury brands can create an environment where buyers feel confident, valued, and validated in their indulgences. Ultimately, it's not just about selling products; it's about cultivating meaningful relationships and enriching the lives of uncompromising consumers.

THINKING DIFFERENTLY

Self-Worth, Personal Achievement,
and Emotional Fulfillment

EVOLVING BUYER PSYCHOLOGY

TODAY'S LUXURY CONSUMERS ARE FAR less focused on impressing others and much more attuned to fulfilling their own personal desires. It's more about them than how much they worry about others and in a good way. They are increasingly motivated by self-reward, authenticity, and emotional satisfaction rather than belonging to an elite group. In fact, elitism for many is a turn off. Understanding this shift is critical for anyone looking to market to this modern luxury audience.

Luxury buyers today are driven by a different set of values. While they still seek high-quality products and experiences, their motivations have become more personal and self-affirming. While it may seem apparent that Millennials and Gen Z see luxury as a form of self-expression and personal well-being rather than a display of status, this doesn't apply to the younger generations alone. I believe most people feel this way. The modern-day luxury buyer approaches purchases from an "I deserve it" mindset, but not rooted in a selfish or vain sort of way. Instead, it comes from a place of self-worth, personal achievement, and the desire for emotional fulfillment.

The good news is this shift has the potential to broaden the luxury market for many brands. Self-expression, authenticity, and treating oneself are often easier sells than the justification required to simply impress others. Consumers want to show who they are, not what they own.

LUXURY BUYER BEHAVIOR

PERSONAL FULFILLMENT OVER IMPRESSING OTHERS

TODAY'S BUYERS ARE MORE INWARDLY focused and concerned with how luxury makes them feel rather than how it looks to others. The notion of "treating oneself" has become a key motivator for luxury purchases. It's not about showing off but about personal reward and achieving a deeper sense of satisfaction and joy.

This shift means that luxury is now more closely associated with self-care, mental well-being, and personal indulgence. This is not relegated just to traditional self-care services like spa treatments either! The same notions of personal fulfillment apply to purchasing luxury goods and gourmet experiences. Yes, that handbag, parfum, or designer dress can be about your wellness. For many, it certainly affects how you feel about yourself, evoking feelings of confidence and deservedness, feeling good, recharged, and personally fulfilled.

More good news! How do today's consumers often respond to challenges in life and even downturns in the economy? They gravitate towards a petit plaisir (or not-so-small pleasure), a special moment, and an escape from reality. They turn to luxury.

AUTHENTICITY AND EMOTIONAL CONNECTION

ALONG WITH PERSONAL FULFILLMENT, TODAY'S luxury buyers also value authenticity. In a world full of mass-produced products, consumers are looking for goods and experiences that are unique, genuine, and reflective of a brand's story. This is a significant departure from the traditional model of luxury, where exclusivity was tied to scarcity.

Authenticity is the new currency of luxury. They want to feel emotionally connected to the brands they support, and they choose those that share their values—such as inclusivity, sustainability, craftsmanship, and social responsibility. They are more likely to buy from a brand that

106

aligns with their beliefs and lifestyle, even if that brand doesn't carry the same allure as traditional luxury labels.

Consumers with discretionary dollars are increasingly using their purchasing power to support brands that are doing good in the world and making them feel good.

◆ IN THE END...

THE MINDSET OF TODAY'S LUXURY buyers has evolved dramatically. Exclusivity, once the foundation of luxury marketing, is no longer the driving force behind affluent consumer behavior. Today's buyers are focused on personal fulfillment, emotional connection, and authenticity. They often approach luxury from an "I deserve it" mindset that is grounded in self-worth, self-care, and self-celebration rather than a simple desire to impress others.

BEYOND DATA
The Critical Role of Behavior, Mindset, and Lifestyle

WHEN IT COMES TO LUXURY marketing, there's often a lot of data, market research, and trend analysis offered. While this information is valuable, it can have its limitations. Data can tell you what products are selling but it cannot capture the nuances of why it resonates with a luxury consumer. It can show you where your customers are coming from but cannot fully explain the journey that led them to your brand. By definition, data and research look in the rear-view mirror. They're built on hindsight and the fast-changing culture and ever-evolving values of the luxury buyer make data and research a bit behind the curve.

The other, far more elusive and nuanced side, is the luxury buyer's behavior, mindset, and lifestyle. Closely monitoring those elements is the most valuable tool you have to stay relevant and in sync with your buyers.

Luxury is not just a product category. Like a plush cashmere robe by Loro Piana, luxury is something to wrap yourself in. It's a chosen lifestyle, an appreciation for beauty and details, and desired experiences. Money alone does not make these decisions. Data does not predict these behaviors. To truly connect with affluent consumers, marketers must go beyond the data and research and delve deep into the psyche of the luxury buyer.

THE BEHAVIOR OF LUXURY BUYERS

LUXURY BUYERS OFTEN EXHIBIT FREQUENT and sudden shifts in behavior, driven by a blend of emotional impulses, evolving priorities, and heightened expectations. One moment, they may seem highly engaged and enthusiastic. The next, they might withdraw or become indecisive. These shifts aren't necessarily about the product or service itself but are often tied to external pressures, fleeting moods, or a sudden change in focus. Luxury buyers live in a world of constant decision fatigue and competing demands, making their behavior less predictable. Understanding this fluidity—and responding with patience, adaptability, and a steady presence—can foster trust and strengthen the relationship.

These often sudden and frequent changes in the behavior of the luxury buyer are worth noting. Pay close attention to changes in behavior and respond accordingly to stay on the winning side.

THE MINDSET OF THE LUXURY CONSUMER

THE MINDSET OF THE LUXURY consumer is another critical factor that data alone cannot capture and—let's be clear—the luxury buyer thinks differently. Or as I point out in my keynotes, when money is not the issue, everything else is.

Affluent buyers have a worldview shaped by their success, experiences, and values. However, this mindset is not static; it evolves with changes in personal circumstances, societal trends, and global events. After every global or national event or crisis, there's always a shift in values. What was once of high value may become less so and money invested can shift in another direction. For example, from showiness to discretion. From consumption to sustainability. And often feels like it shifts overnight.

Luxury consumers are increasingly drawn to companies that are not just selling products but are also telling a story, embodying a philosophy, or championing a cause. In other words, brands that understand their current mindset.

LIFESTYLE AS A MARKETING LEVER

LIFESTYLE IS PERHAPS THE MOST critical element in luxury marketing. The lifestyle of a luxury consumer is not just about how they spend their money; it's about how they live their lives. This includes their social circles, hobbies, travel preferences, and even their media consumption habits. Understanding this lifestyle is key to positioning a brand in a way that resonates deeply with the intended audience.

Always the first advice I give a luxury business owner or luxury brand leader is to embody the life of their customer, even if only in limited experiences or short vignettes at first. You simply cannot fully understand their buying decisions, and what they need to see, hear, and feel until you have seen the world from their perspective. Or walked in their shoes, or Louboutins as the case may be.

By aligning a brand with the lifestyle of its customers, marketers can create a deeper connection, one that goes beyond the superficial and taps into the very essence of how these customers live and who they aspire to be.

◆ IN THE END...

WHILE DATA AND MARKET TRENDS are crucial tools for the luxury marketer, they are not enough on their own. The true power of luxury marketing lies in understanding the behavior, mindset, and lifestyle of the luxury consumer. These are the elements that drive emotional connections, inspire brand loyalty, and create the kind of experiences that luxury buyers crave.

SEEING THEMSELVES

How Self-Perception Plays a Role

A COMMON MISCONCEPTION IN LUXURY branding and marketing is that the sole focus is on the image of the brand. While brand image is important of course, there is another very important consideration—the luxury buyer's self-perception. A luxury brand isn't just about the crafted image of the brand but also how it shapes and reflects how their customers see themselves in the world.

Luxury buyers carefully select the message they want to communicate based on the style, status, and history of any chosen brand. Through the brands they choose, they are carefully curating how they want to be portrayed and—as a portrait photographer for this discerning clientele for forty years—I saw first-hand how important it is to them that they are seen in a way that aligns with their self-image. Every choice, from the brands they wear to the art they collect, is a deliberate statement.

Luxury brands can leverage this by understanding and aligning their brand identity with the self-image of their ideal customers. Since they are building the story of themselves with the luxury brands and services they choose, they will consider various factors.

THE LEVEL OF PRESTIGE

LET'S LOOK AT LUXURY WATCHES as an example. The level of prestige among these luxury brands varies. For example, Patek Philippe, Audemars Piguet, and Breitling are all luxury brand watches but each suggests a different level of prestige. If a buyer feels they must be seen as the most accomplished, most deserving individual, then they are going to purchase the most top-of-the-line brand like Patek Philippe. Another luxury buyer may want to be seen as successful but not too excessive and choose Breitling, whether they can afford the top-of-the-line brand or not.

Even among the narrow niche of luxury goods and services, there are various levels of prestige and buyers will take into consideration how they want to be perceived and the message they are communicating through the brands they choose. In today's world of responsible consumption, luxury brands need to consider this and understand how their ideal customer wants to be perceived.

THE DESERVINGNESS FACTOR

DESERVINGNESS IS A CRUCIAL EMOTIONAL component driving luxury purchases. Luxury buyers often feel they have earned the right to indulge in high-end goods and services. This sense of deservingness is closely linked to their life experiences, struggles, and triumphs. They believe they deserve to reward themselves after overcoming challenges or reaching significant milestones.

In today's climate of self-care, making oneself feel good, and celebrating the moment, the deserving factor is a strong emotional buying trigger. The driving emotions need not be just the big things in life such as a promotion, level of success, or a milestone but everyday rewards for facing down the challenges of life, a strong desire to feel good, and all-around feelings of deservedness. In such contexts, luxury purchases are seen as justified rewards and this writer couldn't agree more! Carpe diem can also mean buy the damn thing!

THE SOCIAL MIRROR

THE CONCEPT OF THE "SOCIAL mirror" suggests that individuals often see themselves as they want others to see them and for some luxury buyers, this is an important consideration. Their social circles and societal perceptions heavily influence their purchasing decisions. Social dynamics play a pivotal role in shaping the behavior of luxury buyers.

To fit in and be recognized as part of the group, individuals may feel compelled to buy high-end goods and services and shop in all the "right" places. This social validation reinforces their self-perception and how they want to be seen in the world. The social mirror effect means that luxury purchases and experiences are not just about personal gratification but also about their self-image. For example, how they want to be seen is often an important consideration in a country club or the gated community one chooses to live in. The choice says a lot about themselves.

BRAND STORY

THE LUXURY BUYER WILL OFTEN also resonate with the history and story of the brands they choose. The story of a brand becomes the story they want to tell about themselves and many luxury brands are masterful at narratives. Riva Yachts frequently references the celebrities and cultural icons who have owned and enjoyed their yachts. This lends aspirational value to the brand, connecting customers to a legacy of celebrity and glamour. Advertising campaigns often feature archival footage or photographs of icons like Sophia Loren or Sean Connery on Riva boats.

Even if a brand isn't rich in history, such as a new luxury service business, sharing the story of the founder, the values on which the business is built, and the reason for the passion behind the service are all stories that the luxury buyer may want to get behind or see themselves in.

A REFLECTION OF VALUES

AS SOCIETY EVOLVES, SO TOO do the values and identities of luxury consumers. For example, the rise of sustainability and ethical consumption is reshaping the luxury landscape. Modern consumers are increasingly associating luxury with values such as environmental responsibility and social impact. Brands like Gucci exemplify sustainable luxury by using eco-friendly materials like regenerated nylon and organic cotton, and with initiatives like Gucci Off The Grid, which uses solely recycled, organic, and bio-based materials.

This evolution underscores the notion that luxury is inherently tied to changing personal values and how individuals see their place in the world. In this case, the modern luxury consumer seeks brands that not only reflect their refined tastes but also their values and beliefs. A luxury brand must be constantly aware of the changing values of their clients.

◆ IN THE END...

WHILE THE IMAGE OF A luxury brand undeniably plays a role in attracting buyers, it is the alignment of the brand's values with the buyer's self-perception that truly seals the deal. Luxury buyers seek brands that resonate with their identity, values, and lifestyle. Shifting the perspective from luxury being about the brand to being about the buyer's self-perception re-directs the focus from the external image of the brand to the internal narrative of the buyer. It is not just about what the brand represents but about how their choice of brand aligns with how they see themselves.

DIANE VON FURSTENBERG
A Step Ahead

DIANE VON FURSTENBERG (DVF) BUILT her brand by truly understanding her customers—modern, professional women who wanted elegance without complication. In 1974, she introduced her now-iconic wrap dress, a simple yet transformative garment that demonstrates her deep understanding of what her clients desired: style that fit seamlessly into their busy lives.

The wrap dress was more than a fashion statement, it was a solution. Its design, easy to put on and take off, resonated with women balancing careers, travel, and family. The vibrant, busy patterns not only added flair but cleverly masked wrinkles, making the dress ideal for packing and wearing on the go. Women could look polished and feel confident with minimal effort—a luxury in itself for the ambitious women DVF served.

Von Furstenberg's pricing strategy was equally thoughtful. Positioned at the low end of high-end fashion, her dresses offered attainable luxury. They allowed her customers to indulge in elegance while feeling smart about their investment. It was a balance of aspiration and practicality, perfectly aligned with her clients' values.

This deep connection to her audience sets DVF apart. She understood not only their aesthetic preferences but also their lifestyles, challenges, and mindsets. Her brand became synonymous with empowerment, while celebrating beauty and independence.

DVF's success is a testament to the power of knowing your customer intimately. By designing for real women with real lives, she created a brand that feels personal, purposeful, and timeless: luxury that truly speaks to its audience.

THE DUAL MINDSET

Discount Luxury and High-End Experiences

MANY LUXURY PROFESSIONALS SEEM TO feel a growing trend has emerged. Luxury buyers are increasingly frequenting luxury discount stores and apps, looking to find their favorite high-end brands for less. However, this is not new behavior at all. I do agree somewhere along the way this dual mindset became more common where luxury buyers would seek discounts while maintaining their affinity for luxury brands. But this is not a new trend. I saw this behavior in my ultra-wealthy photography clients decades ago.

For example, while my clients would choose only the best in consumable foods from the local specialty market, they (or their staff) would head over to Costco, a discount warehouse in the U.S., for the paper goods. I determined this behavior was based on what they valued most and what was a commodity. My family-centric clients cared deeply about what nourished their family. They cared far less about the paper goods. I saw it as a "yes and" behavior more than an "either/or" behavior, so there's no need for luxury brand experiences to worry.

One of the key lessons here for luxury goods and services is not to become a commodity in a world that is constantly commoditizing. Left unchecked, there's always been a natural trend from class to mass. The information age (aka internet) commoditized information, making everything available to everyone. As a high-end family portrait photographer I experienced this firsthand. The transition from film to digital and the development of quality cell phone cameras seemingly put the ability to capture precious family moments in everyone's hands. What's left when the marketplace has become seemingly equalized? You must figure out how to stand out. How to be exceptional.

The good news is I believe this also indicates a constant raising of standards and expectations on the part of consumers. This improves the world. When yesterday's pillar of luxury becomes today's ordinary, could it be perhaps consumers are looking for the next level of what impresses them? Challenge accepted.

As it always has, all of this becomes a call for luxury brands to constantly stay on top of their game in order to stay relevant. This dual mindset of luxury buyers may not be new but neither is the constant need for the definition of luxury to evolve.

It is however worthwhile to look at this seemingly contradictory behavior because it's another example that highlights the complex psychology of luxury buyers. Understanding this dual mindset will be vital for businesses targeting luxury buyers.

THE THRILL OF THE HUNT

LUXURY DISCOUNT OUTLETS LIKE NORDSTROM Rack, Saks Off Fifth, and apps such as Rue La La, Gilt, and Lyst have created a niche for themselves by offering high-end goods at reduced prices. For many luxury buyers, this intersection of affordability and exclusivity is irresistible. One of the strongest psychological triggers for luxury buyers shopping at discount outlets is the thrill of the hunt. These shoppers take pleasure in finding deals on items that would typically be priced much higher. It's about more than just getting something for less; it's the emotional high that comes from feeling like they've outsmarted the system, securing something rare and chic for a fraction of the cost.

It's been said that this sense of accomplishment taps into the same brain functions that gamblers experience when they win at a casino. I can attest to that! For luxury buyers, discount stores and apps create an environment where the thrill is exciting, the rewards are great, and the effort is worth the chase.

JUSTIFICATION OF EXTRAVAGANCE

LET'S FACE IT, HUMANS ARE emotional buyers and we love to justify what we want. Luxury buyers even more so. I believe they justify their larger, more extravagant purchases by offsetting them with bargains. Fortunately, my services were one of their larger purchases and I would often hear them justify the expense away by mentioning where they were going to cut back elsewhere. By purchasing discounted luxury goods, consumers can justify splurging on other expensive items or experiences. This "money swapping" becomes a justification for indulging in even higher-end products or lavish experiences, maintaining the balance between thriftiness and indulgence. The good news is it may keep the same amount of money in circulation, just redistributed. I also think there was a desire to feel they were making smart financial decisions, perhaps to offset the outward appearance or internal conflict that they were feeling about their values.

ACCESSIBLE LUXURY

LUXURY DISCOUNT STORES AND APPS offer an interesting paradox for high-end buyers. While the items are discounted, they're still luxurious, which means they maintain their upscale positioning. Unlike bargain basement stores, luxury outlets feature brands that inherently signal upscale brands. The price might be reduced, but the social value of owning a Chanel handbag or Dolce and Gabbana shirt remains intact.

For luxury buyers, this maintains the aspirational nature of what they pursue while making it attainable. They get to indulge in the luxury brand experience while paying less, striking a balance between exclusivity and accessibility.

◆ IN THE END...

UNDERSTANDING THIS DUAL MINDSET CAN help luxury brands not panic when this complex behavior once again seems to be a new trend and focus instead on raising the bar to keep their brand relevant.

THE LUXURY BUYER PARADOX

How to Blend the Polished with the Personal

WHEN PERFECTION IS NOT JUST an expectation but the standard, it may seem contradictory that high-end clients also deeply value a certain amount of casualness and "realness." The surprise to many not accustomed to serving high-end clients is the broad range of what luxury means to them.

After many years of speaking about the pricing strategies of luxury brands—and how, when shopping in high-end stores, the registers are rarely visible, often tucked in back rooms—I decided to post a photo on social media of a back room at a well-known upscale brand in New York City. I was overwhelmed with the dismay people expressed and the uproar about the condition of the back room. A small trash can sat in view and a step stool was leaning against the wall. Dozens of comments from people exclaimed, "How is this backroom luxury?"

I realized there is a significant misunderstanding about the seemingly paradoxical behavior of the luxury buyer.

I believe this misunderstanding can be best explained as the luxury buyer having a much broader definition of what luxury is to them and what their lives actually look like than many people realize. Especially for the affluent customer who is very accustomed and comfortable with their wealth.

Let's dive deeper into understanding this unexpected behavior of the luxury buyer.

A CRAVING FOR REALNESS

EVEN LUXURY CONSUMERS WHO INHABIT a world of curated perfection long for experiences that feel real and appreciate just "getting down to business." Especially when you show respect for their busy lives, as was the case in the photo I posted on social media. Most often, the sales associate escapes behind a curtain with your items and comes out with your receipt. But in this example, it was the busy holiday season and I was ushered off the long line of one room to a different backroom that was available for immediate checkout. The awareness and respect the sales associate showed those of us in the long line was far more of a luxury than worrying about the perfection of a behind-the-scenes room. Busy luxury buyers highly appreciated knowing when to let the veil of perfection down a bit to get real and get the job done.

TRUST THROUGH TRANSPARENCY

LUXURY BUYERS HIGHLY VALUE TRANSPARENCY and straightforwardness in all their dealings. They appreciate clarity and directness in communication and trust that what they see is what they get. Be upfront and clear about pricing. It's why on high-end goods and services, prices are rounded off—$500 is to the point whereas $497 is silly. They see right through classic and clever sales techniques. They expect transparency about product details, how items are sourced, and quality assuredness. For luxury consumers, honesty is a reflection of brand integrity, reinforcing the perception that they are making an informed, worthwhile investment. Transparency builds trust and lasting relationships, setting luxury brands apart in a competitive market.

INTIMACY AMID PERFECTION

YOU ENJOYED THE FINEST PERFORMANCE on Broadway, savored the most amazing meal at an impossible-to-get-into restaurant, were wowed by the beautiful display of luxury goods. Then, your VIP tickets welcome you backstage, you choose to sit at the chef's table, or you're invited into the backroom to checkout. These are deeply personal experiences that create intimacy amid perfection and are highly valued by purveyors of the finer things in life. Not only is the contrast between front-of-the-house and back-of-the-house compelling, but it speaks to the much broader and highly sophisticated taste of luxury buyers. They appreciate vulnerability and authenticity as much as perfection and performance.

ESCAPE FROM FORMALITY

TO THE SURPRISE OF MANY, luxury buyers often appreciate a break from formality when engaging with luxury goods and service providers because it offers a refreshing contrast to their highly structured world full of expectations. While they value sophistication and professionalism, they also enjoy more authentic, personable interactions that feel human and effortless. A relaxed approach—without sacrificing professionalism—will deepen the brand/customer relationship. While my brand name is Jeffrey Shaw, those that I interact with eventually get to know me as Jeff. It's an intentional strategy toward a more intimate relationship. As a photographer on location in the most beautiful of homes, I knew to dress professionally yet, at the same time, had to be prepared to kneel on the grass to capture the best moment. The contrast and momentarily escaping from the formality creates the deepest and most loyal customer relationships.

◆ IN THE END...

WHILE IT MAY SEEM PARADOXICAL, it's the perfect blend of the polished and the personal that luxury consumers actually crave. The challenge is not to choose between perfection and casualness but to masterfully blend the two. Luxury consumers want to be wowed by the performance, but they also want moments of intimacy and authenticity. Luxury brands and service providers that can seamlessly integrate both of these elements will not only meet their high expectations but also create lasting emotional connections.

THE HIDDEN FEARS
THAT CAN CAUSE HESITATION

WHEN WE THINK OF LUXURY buyers, we often imagine individuals with unlimited resources who make purchases without hesitation or remorse. In reality, the mindset of a luxury buyer is far more complex. Beyond concerns about affordability, luxury buyers grapple with issues of priorities, values, and social dynamics. Let's explore some of the emotions and fears that can cause second-guessing.

FEAR OF EMBARRASSMENT

EVEN THE ULTRA-WEALTHY CAN WORRY about stepping into situations that may lead to embarrassment. One of the reasons for this is that successful individuals tend to have an aspirational mindset. They socialize and work with people at higher levels of wealth or success and strive to reach that next level themselves. "Playing tennis with the better player," as the saying goes. This constant striving drives them to seek higher-end brands, more reputable services, and more extravagant experiences. However, it also creates hesitancy. Luxury buyers can feel uncertain about stepping beyond their current comfort level, causing them to approach purchases cautiously, testing the waters before fully committing.

Another source of hesitation is the reputation of luxury brands or service providers. These reputations can sometimes be exaggerated, creating false perceptions about accessibility. As my own reputation as the family photographer of choice for ultra-high-net-worth individuals (UHNWIs) grew, I noticed how often potential clients hesitated to inquire, assuming my services were unattainable. Many were pleasantly surprised when they learned the actual rates. While this initially seemed positive, I wondered how much business was being lost due to inflated rate perception. Balancing a luxury brand's image with an approachable reality is crucial to prevent misunderstandings and assure luxury buyers that they won't find themselves in an embarrassing situation.

FEAR OF CONFLICTING PRIORITIES

A SIGNIFICANT CONCERN FOR LUXURY buyers is how large financial purchases might conflict with their broader priorities. It's not always a question of affordability but rather how a purchase aligns with their values. Even when money isn't an issue, luxury buyers prioritize different aspects of their lives, whether it's fashion, cars, travel, family, or philanthropy.

For example, someone might be able to afford a lavish vacation home but hesitate because they value traveling the world more than being tied to a single property. In such cases, it's not the cost that holds them back, but the fear that the purchase might conflict with their deeper desires for freedom or exploration.

Luxury buyers often ask themselves, "Does this purchase align with what's truly important to me?" If the answer is no, they may walk away, regardless of their financial capability.

FEAR OF PERCEPTION

SOCIAL DYNAMICS PLAY A SIGNIFICANT role in the hesitation of luxury buyers. Even among the affluent, wealth, success, and spending habits are scrutinized. Perhaps even more so. The fear of being perceived as wasteful or frivolous weighs heavily on the minds of luxury consumers. Many wealthy individuals feel pressure to justify their purchases to friends, family, their children, or business associates, especially in a society where being smart with your money is highly valued.

This pressure is particularly relevant in today's market, where sustainability and conscientious consumerism are becoming increasingly important. Luxury buyers are often mindful of how their purchases may be perceived by others, both in terms of extravagance and social responsibility. They want to project an image of being aligned with broader values and may hesitate if they feel that a purchase might contradict that image.

FEAR OF BUYER'S REMORSE

EVEN THE WEALTHIEST INDIVIDUALS CAN experience buyer's remorse. The stakes may be different, but the emotions are the same. Wealthy buyers may worry that a luxury item, no matter how rare or beautiful, won't bring the satisfaction they seek or will sit unused once the initial excitement fades.

For example, someone might buy a yacht, only to realize they don't have enough time to enjoy it. What once seemed like a dream purchase can quickly become a burden trying to maintain it. The fear of regretting such a significant purchase often holds buyers back, even if it was originally a dream come true.

◆ IN THE END...

IN SOME WAYS, THE WORLD of luxury buyers may be more similar to mid-scale and average buyers than initially thought. They have fears too and these fears of embarrassment, conflicting priorities, perception, and buyer's remorse significantly influence the decision-making process of luxury buyers. Even though they may have the resources to purchase almost anything, they approach each purchase cautiously, weighing the emotional and other consequences as much as the financial cost. Even the wealthiest individuals experience hesitation and fear when making high-end purchases. Their concerns stem not just from affordability but from deeper issues related to their priorities, being smart with their money, and the fear of regret.

For those serving the luxury market, understanding and addressing these hidden fears is essential to really serving high-end clients. By emphasizing trust, value, and respect for their broader concerns, brands and service providers can help luxury buyers feel confident in their decisions, alleviating some of their fears.

MINDSET OVER DEMOGRAPHICS

ONE OF THE THINGS I love when speaking at a conference is watching the attendees experience what I refer to as a fundamental shift: when something so obvious and instinctively known suddenly becomes clear. It sort of "drops in" as I like to say. Here's one such idea.

When marketing to the luxury buyer, it's more important to focus on their mindset than demographics.

This concept is both obvious and frequently overlooked. In the world of luxury marketing, it's easy to fall into the trap of focusing on specific demographics. You instinctively know that demographics is just a piece of the puzzle but suddenly it becomes the main focus. Consider the amount of conversation about market trends and demographics on LinkedIn and other outlets. Useful information, but I stand by my core belief that nothing is ever more important than understanding mindset and buyer psychology.

Conventional wisdom tells us to identify age, income level, occupation, and geographical location. However, the reality of selling to the affluent is far more nuanced, and paying attention to their ever-evolving mindset can keep a brand far more current and adaptable than trends and demographics. While I most often focus on emotional drivers, understanding mindset drivers is ever so slightly different yet no less important.

Demographics are inherently limiting when applied too rigidly. They categorize people into narrow groups, potentially overlooking the broader market. A sixty-year-old UHNWI (ultra-high-net-worth individual) and a thirty-year-old entrepreneur may be in the market for the same luxury goods and services, rendering typical demographics useless in understanding how a brand might speak to each of these audiences differently and appeal to both.

In the world of luxury, mindset eclipses demographics. Focusing on the mindset more than demographics opens the door to a wider, more accurate understanding of who your potential customers might be. It's expansive thinking versus limited thinking.

MARKETING TO THEIR MINDSET

TO EFFECTIVELY MARKET TO THE luxury buyer, you need to shift your focus from who the buyer is to what emotionally drives them. This requires a deep understanding of their values, aspirations, and desires. Here are some strategies to consider:

1. **Create Resonance:** Tell your brand story. The why, the heritage, the purpose, and the mission behind the luxury brand that aligns with the luxury buyer's values and desires. This story goes beyond the product or service to how it fits into the buyer's lifestyle. This is what I refer to as understanding their self-perception. It's understanding how your customers see themselves, want to see themselves, or want to be seen by others and aligning your story with the story they want to tell. Consistency across all touchpoints from advertising to customer service is crucial to maintaining this narrative.

2. **Make Them Feel Special:** Whether it's through invite-only events, offers available only to them, special access, or limited opportunities, make them feel like they are part of a special club. When marketing to the mindset more than the demographic, that doesn't mean making them feel special has to feel exclusive.

It needs to make them feel separate from the masses and that's a true desire for the luxury buyer, no matter the demographic. I spoke once to an association of luxury suite directors, yes—the people in charge of private box seats at sports and entertainment arenas. One of my goals was to shift the marketing thinking from luxury suites being a choice only for corporations out to impress their clients to realize the untapped market for affluent individuals who simply want separation from the masses. More often than not, you'll find folks enjoying a sporting event from a luxury suite in t-shirts and shorts rather than suits. The mindset is the desire for ease and separation across a broad demographic.

3. **Don't Put Them in a Box:** This is where focusing on demographics too strongly can go all wrong. No one wants to be typecast or put into a box. When focusing too much on demographics, it can be easy to make assumptions. This often happens in luxury retail when sales associates assume who can and can't afford their products and services based on a pre-established demographic. You simply don't know anyone's story until you do. Luxury buyers expect an openness and a high level of personalized treatment without any preconceived notions. Today's buyers will often challenge assumptions. Marketing messages and customer interactions should be geared to reflect the unique preferences and interests of each customer without any assumptions. Express the deep desires, values, and aspirations of ideal buyers and let them identify for themselves whether they fit into the box you're offering rather than make anyone feel like it is being decided for them whether they fit into a box or not.

4. **Brand Image and Message Is the Attractor and Filter:** Invest in high-quality content that speaks the lingo of your ideal customer

and reflects the premium nature of your brand. My book, *LINGO,* provides a five-step process to unpack the lingo of ideal clients and build the brand message that speaks to them. This includes everything from website design to social media posts. Visual content should be polished and sophisticated, while written content should be elegant and articulate. The goal is to create an immersive brand experience that feels luxurious at every touch-point and makes the ideal luxury buyer feel like, "Hey, they are speaking to me," regardless of the demographic. If it speaks to them, it speaks to them.

◆ IN THE END...

MINDSET IS EVERYTHING. IN THE world of luxury marketing, demographics alone are not enough. To truly resonate with the affluent buyer, you must understand and appeal to their mindset as well as their heartfelt emotions. This means recognizing the importance of creating resonance, making them feel special, not putting them in a box, and building a brand message that speaks to them. It's not just about who they are; it's also about how they think.

NET-A-PORTER

Meeting Your Customers Where They Are

IN MANHATTAN IN THE EARLY 2000s, I took note of a brand emerging with a unique business model. They clearly understood their upscale clientele up and down Park, Madison, and Fifth Avenue.

Recognizing the challenges of Manhattan life—tight schedules, crowded streets, and the constant search for convenience—Net-a-Porter introduced a service that transformed the traditional shopping experience for luxury shoppers. Customers could select multiple dresses online and have them delivered directly to their apartments. This approach allowed clients to try on the clothes at home with access to their wardrobes and the privacy of their personal space. It eliminated the guesswork of imagining how a piece might look in real life or whether it would pair well with their accessories.

The service went a step further by offering effortless returns. Unwanted items could be left with the doorman for easy pickup, removing the need for customers to visit a store. For New York's elite, juggling demanding careers, social lives, and traffic, this seamless approach provided an invaluable time-saving benefit.

By essentially bringing a luxury boutique to the customer's doorstep, Net-a-Porter demonstrated its deep understanding of its clients' priorities. The initiative not only reflected the brand's commitment to exceptional service but also illustrated how luxury can evolve with technology to enhance personalization and convenience. It's a shining example of how premium brands can creatively meet consumers' needs while retaining the prestige of luxury by taking the time to really understand those they serve.

UNEXPECTED KINDNESSES

I WAS RECENTLY INSPIRED BY a story about an act of kindness shared with me about a fitness club owner in Palm Beach, Florida. Something I've seen many times over my career: unexpected kindness. It's kindness when there was no expectation, and really underscored the character of the people we can be so fortunate to work with.

To defray rising costs, this fitness club owner needed to increase fees at his facility and for private training sessions for his high-end clientele. His first thought was to increase monthly dues which I discouraged, suggesting it might feel like nickel and diming since it wasn't a large amount of money for his upscale clientele. Instead, I suggested he implement a one-time annual membership fee in addition to his club's monthly dues. This way it felt worthy of the conversation and it was a one-time increase instead of a monthly reminder of a small amount of increase.

To honor a few of his most loyal clients, he chose to waive the newly enacted annual fee. He was shocked at the number of clients from this select group that refused the waiver and insisted on paying the new fee. Imagine, you're doing the right thing by acknowledging the longstanding business from a client and they refuse the favor!

At first glance, this might seem counterintuitive or even frivolous, especially when the luxury buyer is so often accused of acting entitled or looking for the best deal even when they can afford it. But such kindness is actually not atypical of the wealthiest of clients. Unexpected, yes, but not entirely surprising.

Having experienced such acts of kindness myself far more many times that any attitudes of entitlement, I thought it was fair to share the very kind, altruistic side of the luxury buyer and perhaps some of the reasoning behind it.

THEY WANT YOU TO SUCCEED

WHILE OTHER REASONS FOR ACTS of kindness and generosity may be more subtle, the most straightforward reason may be they simply want a business to succeed. Particularly if you provide a service they value, have a relationship with you and your business, and want to be assured your service continues to be available for themselves and others. In this case, they want their trainer to be there for them and succeed. He's proven himself to be a valuable part of their lives and all indications are they have a strong bond.

Also, because they themselves likely worked hard to achieve their success, or at least maintain it, the luxury buyer tends to value the hard work they know goes into building and sustaining a business. They want you to succeed and would prefer to fully financially support your business instead of accepting a break, particularly in a time of need.

RESPECT AND QUALITY

AS BUYERS OF THE FINEST products and services, luxury clients recognize that superior craftsmanship, rare materials, and meticulous service are not accidental but the result of dedication and a commitment to excellence. Discounting, in their eyes, risks undermining the quality they are accustomed to, whether it's the precision of a hand-stitched leather bag or enough staff to provide a seamless experience.

They value professionals who operate with precision, attentiveness, and a deeply personalized touch. Whether it's a private chef preparing an exquisite multi-course meal or a trusted advisor managing their financial portfolios, these clients understand that exceptional service requires expertise, preparation, and support. Paying full price, then, becomes a gesture of respect and an acknowledgment they appreciate the value they're receiving. They want this level of quality and service preserved for future experiences and are willing to pay for it.

UPHOLDING BRAND IMAGE AND INTEGRITY

LUXURY BRANDS ARE BUILT ON the foundation of superior quality and brand image. These attributes are closely tied to their pricing strategies. When a luxury buyer insists on paying full price, they help uphold the brand's integrity and image, perhaps an image that's important to their own. Discounts can sometimes dilute a brand's image and perceived value and make it seem less special.

By refusing discounts, luxury buyers ensure that the brand retains its premium status, benefiting all who value its unique position in the market. Their intention in generously refusing a discount may be to help preserve the brand's integrity and show kindness not just to the brand, but to other consumers who appreciate and aspire to have a similar experience with the luxury brand or service.

DEMONSTRATING FINANCIAL RESPONSIBILITY

FOR MANY LUXURY BUYERS, THE decision to refuse a discount stems from a place of financial responsibility and respect for the value of money. These individuals understand that the price they pay reflects the true worth of the service or product, including the costs associated with overhead, high-quality materials, and skilled labor. By paying full price, they show respect for the intrinsic value of money.

This mindset extends to a broader societal level. When affluent consumers willingly pay full price, they help contribute to a thriving economy. I have heard buyers (and admittedly have joked myself) that acts of overspending are supporting the economy. Perhaps said in jest, there's some truth and good intention to this. When an economy stagnates, getting it moving can often be the best solution and those that can, often do.

ENCOURAGING FAIR WAGES AND ETHICAL PRACTICES

INCREASINGLY AND QUITE THANKFULLY, LUXURY buyers can have a keen interest in ethical consumerism. They are often very aware of the production practices behind the goods they purchase. By paying full price, they are more likely to support brands that provide fair wages, maintain ethical working conditions, and practice environmental sustainability. This conscious choice can drive positive change in many industries, encouraging brands to uphold higher ethical standards.

This form of kindness extends beyond the immediate transaction. It influences industries to prioritize fair treatment of workers, sustainable practices, and ethical sourcing of materials. Luxury buyers who refuse discounts are indirectly promoting a more equitable and responsible market, benefiting countless individuals involved in the production chain.

◆ IN THE END...

LUXURY BUYERS WHO REFUSE DISCOUNTS often do so with a sense of responsibility and generosity. They set an example for others, demonstrating that wealth can be used to support and uplift and not just for financial gain. Their actions reflect a willingness to contribute positively to the economic and social fabric of society. Through their actions, luxury buyers can show that kindness can be a powerful force in the world of consumerism.

DEALING WITH DIFFICULT CUSTOMERS
Understanding Them, Yourself, and What to Do About It

THE MOMENT I ANNOUNCED I was writing this book, I received inquiries as to whether I would be addressing the issue of dealing with difficult clients because "wealthy people are often so difficult to work with." It was not my intention to address this topic at all because I have a strong aversion to the judgments and assumptions underlying this belief. My immediate response was, "Let's start by not stereotyping that wealthy people are difficult because if that's your perspective, you can't be surprised that's what you're getting back."

But I did decide it's a helpful topic to address and will do so in my typical fashion—addressing what might be your role as a luxury service provider and how can you get the results you want—and because there will be some difficult customers, wealthy or not, some practical ideas to deal with the situation.

Wealth does not equate to difficulty. Instead, looking from a perspective of empathy and understanding, you will see that their wealth and social standing often bring added layers of complexity to their personal and professional life, such as juggling extraordinary demands, a family life that is like a business in and of itself, the duality of appearances, and more. By recognizing this, luxury service providers have an opportunity to rise to a higher standard, delivering not only the expected service but also demonstrating a remarkable depth of understanding.

UNDERSTANDING THEM AND THEIR LIVES: THE COMPLEX LIVES OF LUXURY CLIENTS

IT'S EASY TO PAINT AN image of the wealthy client as overly particular and demanding, even difficult. This impression, however, misses a deeper truth. Many affluent clients are juggling extraordinary demands on their time, emotional energy, and financial resources. Their lives might appear seamless from the outside, yet they are managing complexities that most of us will never encounter.

For some, their estates and households operate like small corporations. They employ staff, oversee events, manage multiple properties, and coordinate numerous professional and social responsibilities. This high level of organization is essential, not indulgent, to meet the demands of their lives. Just as with any individual balancing a demanding career and personal life, affluent clients often seek service providers who can help relieve some of this weight from professionals who understand, and accommodate, the sheer magnitude of what they're carrying. Yes, the weight they are carrying can sometimes boil over to appearing difficult, but if you understand this fundamental truth of their lives, you can receive the added pressure with greater understanding, consider it less of a personal attack, and if possible, alleviate some of the weight, for which they will be very grateful.

THE DUALITY OF THE LUXURY CLIENT'S LIFE

WHILE IT'S TRUE THAT LUXURY buyers enjoy the finer things in life, their lives also include struggles and sacrifices that are often overlooked. For many affluent individuals, the gap between appearances and their reality can create a greater than typical dissonance that can be very difficult for them to manage. They may work tirelessly to cultivate the perfect life, lead successful businesses, sustain philanthropic projects, and support family and friends through challenging times, all while managing the same human experiences—of grief, loss, family dynamics, aging parents, and troubled teens—that the rest of us face. However, the gap between their reality and their appearances can be far greater. Emotionally, on a human level, this gap is very difficult to manage.

This reality can leave luxury clients feeling as if they live in two extreme worlds: the one they present to the world and the one they experience internally. This duality brings added pressure, intensifying the already weighty responsibilities they bear. And sometimes they may not manage this dissonance very well. They are humans having a very human experience, just like everyone else. By approaching them with understanding, luxury service providers can become a grounding, compassionate presence who genuinely listens and sees beyond the surface to the real, struggling human just making it through this thing called life.

WHAT YOU CAN DO: SET ASIDE ASSUMPTIONS

START BY SETTING ASIDE PRECONCEPTIONS about "difficult" or "demanding" behavior. When affluent clients ask for high standards, it doesn't mean they are coming from a place of entitlement. Their expectation for quality and service often stems from a desire for consistent standards and trust, as they seek professionals who can reliably uphold the level of care they require. It takes a commitment to see beyond the stereotypes and approach clients with the curiosity and kindness needed to build true rapport. By setting aside assumptions and embracing an empathetic approach, luxury providers have the chance to create interactions that respect the lives of their clients while elevating their own professionalism. Remember, how you see the world is how the world sees you. Make it a practice to put into the world exactly what you want to receive in return.

CONSIDER IT YOUR CALL TO GREATNESS

ULTIMATELY, WORKING WITH AFFLUENT CLIENTS is an invitation for you as a service provider to step up your own call to greatness. It's an opportunity to listen attentively, speak candidly, and genuinely serve their unique needs. Providing exceptional service to this clientele is more than a transaction—it's a partnership. It's about understanding their lives and supporting them in ways that genuinely matter. Every interaction is an opportunity to connect with empathy, respect, and a clear-eyed view of their unique pressures and ambitions. By choosing to view affluent clients through this lens, service providers can rise to a higher level of service and find in themselves more than they ever could have imagined. The privilege of working with affluent clients comes with an invitation to grow, not only in skill and delivery, but in character. It's a reminder that wealth does not shield anyone from the trials and complexities of life. This compassionate approach isn't just good business, it's the true mark of greatness.

WHEN EMPATHY AND UNDERSTANDING AREN'T ENOUGH

BEING IN THE PUBLIC ARENA as a luxury service provider does mean on occasion that no matter what you do—even having a deep understanding of their lives, and mustering up all the greatness in yourself you can— simply won't be enough. Again, I believe this has more to do with the amount of exposure you may face than it has to do with any socio-economic group.

But there will be customers that are simply difficult. Here are some ways to manage challenging clients while maintaining a professional and healthy relationship:

- **Set Clear Expectations from the Start**
  Clearly define what clients can expect from you and your service from the onset. If needed, determine this in a contract to allow both parties to refer back to it if expectations shift over time. Transparency helps clients understand not only what they'll

receive but also what is outside of the standard scope, establishing a respectful foundation from the beginning.

- **De-escalate with Empathy**

  When clients are upset or acting unreasonably, validating their feelings can sometimes be enough to de-escalate the situation. Responding empathetically doesn't mean conceding; it shows you're listening and willing to address reasonable concerns. Understand also that often, "difficult" behavior comes from underlying stressors unrelated to you. A calm, empathetic approach may help you understand and address any actual concerns without taking reactions personally.

- **Set Boundaries**

  You can't fault anyone for crossing a boundary if the boundary wasn't clearly stated in the first place. Be sure to set clear communication boundaries, such as when and how they can expect to reach you. If a client request goes beyond the scope of work, say something like, "I'm committed to providing the best service possible, and to do that, I'll need to keep our focus on [defined boundaries]." If a request falls outside your role, respond with a firm yet respectful "No," followed by offering an alternative. For example, "That's outside my scope, but I'd be happy to suggest a resource that could help."

- **The Client Is Not Always Right**

  No provider should tolerate any form of abuse. When you have exercised as much empathy as you can and are still facing strong opposition, make it clear that any form of verbal or physical mistreatment will not be tolerated. If a client crosses into disrespect or aggression, calmly state that such behavior is unacceptable and terminate the working relationship. The customer is most definitely not always right and while some, such as a sales associate, may face consequences from an employer, your self-respect and emotional safety comes first.

- **Fire When Necessary**

    Yes, on a very rare occasion, we may have to fire a client. If a client repeatedly disregards boundaries, consider providing an exit option with diplomacy, such as, "It seems like my services may not be the right fit for what you're looking for. I'd be happy to recommend someone else who might better suit your needs." It's always acceptable to part ways with clients who threaten your well-being or the quality of your work. Ending a relationship thoughtfully preserves both your reputation and your peace of mind.

◆ IN THE END...

LETTING GO OF ASSUMPTIONS, GAINING empathy by understanding their lives, and considering the opportunity for personal growth will likely ward off almost all ill-fated situations. Yet, on occasion, a difficult client may present themselves. One other thing to consider—if there seems to be a pattern of difficult clients over time or a cluster of difficult clients during a particular time, consider the source. It could be a type of client you are attracting that is not aligned with your values. And the source could also be you. I know that when I have gone through some challenging personal times—perhaps my patience was limited, or my attitude was less than ideal—I tended to have more difficult customer interactions. Which of course only worsens one's attitude and so on. So always look inward for what might need to be shifted to see a different result. What's essential is cultivating a practice where your values and standards are non-negotiable, benefiting you and your clients alike.

ELEMENT IV

Luxury Branding

Luxury branding is about creating a world that buyers want to step into, and more importantly, want to see themselves belonging to.

LUXURY BRANDING
Introduction

BRANDING IN THE LUXURY MARKET is more than a beautiful logo or a carefully curated Instagram feed. While they all play a part, it's more than the right color palette, elegant fonts, and premium packaging. In the luxury space, branding is everything. It's the sum of every interaction, every impression, and every emotion that the brand evokes. It's everything a brand puts out into the world that triggers the emotions their customers want to feel. It's the unspoken dialogue between the brand and its audience, a silent yet profoundly powerful connection that transcends the obvious.

Luxury branding is about creating a world that buyers want to step into, and more importantly, want to see themselves belonging to. It's not just about selling products or services; it's about selling identity, aspiration, validation, and belonging. A luxury brand represents a way of life, a sense of purpose, and a reflection of the buyer's self-perception.

The core of luxury branding lies in understanding the buyer at an emotional level. A luxury purchase isn't driven by logic or necessity; it's fueled by how it makes the buyer feel. It's deeply tied to their identity and their sense of self in the world. A luxury brand must speak in a way that resonates with these emotions, in a way that whispers, "You belong here. This is who you are." It's this emotional resonance that differentiates a luxury brand from others and builds an enduring connection.

Luxury branding is about storytelling. But this isn't just any story and certainly not just the story of the brand. It's the buyer's story. Luxury brands don't simply market their history or heritage, they control a narrative that places the buyer at the center. It's about how wearing that piece of jewelry, staying at that resort, the design of their home, or driving that car transforms the buyer's sense of self. It's about the moments of pride, the sense of achievement, and the feelings of deservedness the brand evokes.

The strength of a luxury brand lies in its ability to reflect the values and aspirations of its audience while maintaining its own unique identity. This delicate balance is where the magic happens. A luxury brand must remain relevant without compromising its legacy. It's about remaining fresh and modern while maintaining the standards and reputation that make it timeless. Kind of like a dance between innovation and tradition, where neither steps on the other's toes but both move together in perfect harmony.

What sets luxury branding apart is its role as both an attractor and a filter. A well-executed luxury brand doesn't try to appeal to everyone. Quite the opposite actually. It's unapologetically specific, speaking directly to its ideal audience and signaling it's not for everyone but about being everything to the right someone.

When branding is done right in the luxury market, it becomes a magnetic force. It draws in customers who see themselves in the brand's story, who feel that their own values align with what the brand represents. At the same time, it gently but firmly discourages those who aren't a fit. This isn't about exclusion for the sake of snobbery—it's about reserving space and energy by creating a deep and authentic connection with the people who truly resonate with the brand.

Branding in the luxury market is the gateway to the experience the customer can expect. It sets the tone, builds anticipation, and ensures consistency at every step of the journey. Whether a buyer is scrolling through social media, browsing a website, or stepping into a flagship store, the branding should evoke the same emotions and tell the same story. This seamless consistency isn't just a nice-to-have; it's essential to building trust and loyalty in the luxury market.

This emotional depth is why luxury branding is so much more than what people see. It's not just about looking expensive or high-end. It's about making the buyer feel understood, valued, and inspired. It's about creating a sense of belonging and speaking their lingo, as is the core message of my first book, *LINGO: Discover Your Ideal Customer's Secret Language and Make Your Business Irresistible*. While not written specifically for the luxury market, the core message of the book is an important lesson for luxury providers. We must speak the "secret language" of ideal customers that resonates deeply with their desires, values, and dreams. Their worlds are more secretive and we must build brands that speak to them, consciously and unconsciously.

One of the most overlooked aspects of luxury branding is its role in shaping the buyer's perception of themselves. It's not just about how the buyer sees the brand. It's about how the buyer sees themselves in relation to the brand or how they aspire to be seen. Luxury branding is about projecting an image, a mindset, and a lifestyle. For one buyer, a luxury brand might represent understated elegance and quiet confidence. For another, it might symbolize boldness, creativity, and individuality. The key is that the brand allows buyers to see themselves in its world, aligning with their aspirations and reflecting their identity back to them.

Lastly, luxury branding is never static. The world is constantly changing, and luxury buyers are among the first to respond to these shifts. A luxury brand must remain attuned to these changes, continuously evolving to stay relevant while maintaining its core identity. It's about listening, adapting, and leading and showing buyers that the brand understands their world and is ready to grow alongside them.

In the luxury market, branding isn't just a marketing tool—it's the very soul of the business and the lifestyle of its buyers. It's the emotions it stirs, the aspirations it fuels, and the connections it builds. It's the frontline attractor of ideal customers and the filter for those who don't resonate. It's not surface-level. It's deeply personal, profoundly emotional, and endlessly powerful. Luxury branding is, quite simply, everything.

LEGACY

A Guiding Light for Luxury Brands

ONCE, WHILE PLANNING A TRIP to Paris for a significant birthday, I noticed something striking about my itinerary. It wasn't just about sightseeing or dining at fine restaurants. Instead, it felt like a pilgrimage to the sacred grounds of luxury, a journey to the original locations of iconic brands. Louboutin, Dior, Ladurée—each stop wasn't just a destination but a respectful nod into the legacy of these brands. Even newer names, like fashion brand AMI by Alexandre Mattiussi, drew me in, especially the original location where it all began, steeped in the stories that defined its essence.

This trip wasn't just about indulgence. It became a reflective moment, coinciding with my thoughts about my own legacy. Legacy, I realized, isn't confined to the past or what we leave behind; it's an active force. For luxury brands, legacy is a compass pointing both home and forward. Like a lighthouse, it protects, guides, and illuminates the way ahead.

As we look to the future, I believe legacy will increasingly shape the narrative and trajectory of luxury brands. Legacy is becoming more important than ever, not just as a historical badge of honor but as a living, breathing organism that resonates with today's consumers. It's not just about logos or recognizable trademarks. It's about the emotional connection, the storytelling, and the authenticity that legacy brings.

LEGACY AS CONNECTION

AT ITS CORE, LEGACY CREATES connection. Today's luxury buyers seek more than a product or service. They crave an emotional bond with the luxury brands and services they choose. Luxury isn't just about excellence, it's about identity. Rimowa luggage, a Van Cleef necklace, a home designed by a renowned designer, all tell a story, not just about the brand but also about the consumer.

Whether you're an established name like Hermès or an emerging designer like AMI, your legacy bridges the gap between brand and buyer. It allows consumers to see themselves in your story, to align their values with yours, and to express those values outwardly. Legacy transforms a transaction into an intimate connection, a moment of shared meaning.

This connection is particularly important for younger luxury buyers who often seek brands that reflect their commitment to sustainability, innovation, and social responsibility. A brand's legacy can embody these values, creating an enduring bond with its audience.

LEGACY WITH INNOVATION

For luxury brands, legacy doesn't mean clinging to the past. Instead, it provides the foundation to innovate without losing the essence of the brand. Legacy shouldn't be a limitation, but instead viewed as a launching pad.

Even the most established luxury brands, steeped in history and tradition, must embrace innovation, especially in the digital realm, to remain relevant in today's fast-evolving market. As I often say, you can't stop a moving train and advancements in technology are always moving forward. By leveraging technology such as augmented reality for virtual try-ons, personalized AI-driven shopping experiences, or immersive storytelling through social media and digital campaigns, legacy brands can reach new audiences while staying true to their roots. These efforts should not be seen as departures from a brand's heritage but extensions of it—showing that even in a modern, fast-paced world, legacy brands can evolve without losing their timeless luxury.

LEGACY AS A STORY

LEGACY AND STORYTELLING GO HAND in hand. A brand's story isn't just an anecdote, it's the backbone of its identity. Whether it's the tale of the founder or a rich lineage passed down through generations, storytelling engages buyers on a deeply emotional level.

While well-known legacy brands, such as Dior, Rolls Royce, and Veuve Clicquot have long and historic stories to tell, for emerging brands, storytelling is equally critical. It allows them to craft a legacy even in the absence of long-standing history. Sharing the why behind the passion of the founder or the intended impact of the brand gives buyers a reason to care. Storytelling becomes a way to invite buyers into the brand's journey, making them part of something bigger than a purchase.

LEGACY SHAPES THE FUTURE

AS I REFLECT ON LEGACY, it's clear that it isn't just about leaving your mark. It's very much alive. For established brands, legacy provides stability in an ever-changing world. It reassures buyers that no matter how trends shift, the brand's commitment to quality, craftsmanship, and authenticity remains unwavering.

But legacy also has forward momentum. It's not about nostalgia for what was, it's about honoring the past while shaping the future. Heritage brands don't just rest on their laurels, they evolve. They reinterpret their legacy through modern lenses, ensuring their relevance for new generations.

For newer brands, the challenge is to build a legacy from scratch. But the opportunity is just as great. By staying true to their values and creating compelling stories and legacies, these brands can establish themselves as future icons.

◆ IN THE END...

LEGACY IS THE SOUL OF luxury. It connects the past, present, and future in a way that no other element can. It's the thread that weaves stories, values, and emotions into a tapestry of elegance and excellence. For brands navigating the ever-changing luxury market, legacy isn't just a north star, it's a guiding light.

JO MALONE
A Defining Brand

THROUGH DECADES OF EXPERIENCE CAPTURING family photographs in stunning homes, one detail became strikingly predictable: the presence of Jo Malone products in almost every bathroom. Whether it was a softly glowing candle on a marble vanity or a perfectly arranged collection of lotions in a spa-like bathroom, Jo Malone was an almost permanent fixture in the most exquisite homes. This isn't by chance—it's a testament to the brand's unique ability to resonate with luxury buyers.

Jo Malone has mastered the art of subtle luxury. Its cream-and-black packaging blends seamlessly into a multitude of high-end interiors, exuding elegance without demanding attention. This understated aesthetic appeals to affluent homeowners who value refinement over ostentation, allowing Jo Malone products to elevate a space without overpowering it in both aesthetics and fragrance.

Jo Malone has beautifully positioned itself not simply as a fragrance brand but as a lifestyle companion. Their products don't just scent a home—they set a mood. From the fresh simplicity of Lime Basil & Mandarin to the warmth of Pomegranate Noir (my personal favorite), each fragrance creates an ambiance of sophistication and relaxation, enhancing the sense of luxury that defines these spaces.

Seeing Jo Malone repeatedly in the most beautiful homes underscores its role as a trusted symbol of elegance and good taste. For affluent buyers, Jo Malone is part of the experience of living beautifully. It's no wonder the brand feels as much an element in the home as the home's breathtaking decor.

HOW TO ACHIEVE INCLUSIVITY WITHOUT SACRIFICING EXCLUSIVITY

WITH GREAT CONCERN, I'M OFTEN asked how a luxury brand can maintain exclusivity when it also has a responsibility to society to be inclusive. If luxury goods and services are "not for everyone," how do we not be offensive to someone? In a purely practical sense, no business is for everyone. As is often said, if your business is for everyone, you're really for no one.

How then do we stand out as a luxury brand, knowing our specific ideal clientele, without being tone-deaf to the need for inclusivity?

This is a delicate balancing act luxury brands must figure out to stay relevant and thriving.

In the past, the allure of exclusivity has been a driving force behind the image of a luxury brand. However, as societal values continue to evolve, the challenge lies in striking a delicate balance between maintaining their aura of exclusivity while also embracing inclusivity. It's no longer enough for luxury goods and services to cater only to a select few elite consumers. They must also demonstrate a commitment to diversity and inclusivity in a socially conscious marketplace.

Here are just a few ways that today's luxury goods and service providers can achieve what we hope will be a respectful balance between separating the brand from the masses and not making others feel excluded.

CHOICE OF EXPERIENCES

LUXURY BRANDS CAN OFFER A choice of experiences. Sort of a choose-your-own-adventure. By putting the power of choice in the hands of the consumer, you can reduce feelings of exclusion. This can include a range of service options or access. On one hand, it can involve creating unique and personalized experiences for those customers that choose them, such as VIP events and more private experiences. Yet it can also include what still feels like private access to behind-the-scenes tours of a luxury brand's legacy or direct access to sales associates and support staff to a broader range of customers. Acknowledgment that you are seen can go a long way. By offering a range of experiences, luxury brands can make all customers feel valued and special, regardless of their buying power at that time.

EXPAND OFFERINGS

WHEREAS IN THE PAST, LUXURY brands may have had limited offerings, like bespoke or couture, they can also embrace inclusivity by expanding their product offerings to cater to a more diverse range of consumers—goods and services that are available across a broader price range.

While known as the go-to portrait photographer available for a limited number of sessions per year, traveling to gorgeous places to meet my clients, I also occasionally choose one location to make myself available and invited a broader range of customers for shorter, more affordable portrait sessions. Often in part as a fundraiser for a good cause. I would do several sessions in a day in one location, often not open to the general public, thereby making myself accessible to more people. Providing access to an otherwise private location gave everyone an exclusive experience even though the offering was inclusive. Honestly, it was always one of my favorite things to do and highly appreciated.

Think also about how many designer clothing brands, solely couture in the past, came out with product lines available to the masses in department stores. Of course, this has to be done very carefully so as not to ruin the brand image, but it can be done.

MARKETING REPRESENTATION

LUXURY BRANDS NEED TO TAKE far more care in representing diversity in their marketing efforts. Truthfully, I believe this is an area that a great deal more effort needs to be enacted. This includes a broader representation of body sizes and shapes, skin tones, ethnicities, ages, and sexual identities and representation of various relationships in their advertising campaigns, websites, and public displays. By embracing diversity in their marketing efforts and in all outreach, luxury brands can demonstrate their commitment to inclusivity while expanding their customer.

SOCIAL INITIATIVES

LUXURY BRANDS CAN LEVERAGE THEIR influence and resources to support causes and initiatives that promote inclusivity and diversity. This can involve partnering with nonprofit organizations that support marginalized communities, sponsoring diversity-focused events and initiatives, or launching philanthropic campaigns that address social issues such as racial inequality or LGBTQ+ rights. By aligning themselves with causes that resonate with their values and beliefs, luxury brands can demonstrate their commitment to making a positive impact on society.

But please, a word of caution. Such efforts have to be done with a genuine desire to care about each initiative. When thought of as a checked box of inclusivity, it will be felt that way and do more harm than good. And I don't mean just harm to the brand. Such disingenuous behavior is of no service to society.

◆ IN THE END...

THE BALANCE BETWEEN INCLUSIVITY AND maintaining a luxury brand's positioning is very delicate. But as always, luxury brands are held to a higher standard and this is an opportunity to be strong leaders of a society that is respectful to all.

MORE THAN JUST A HIGH NUMBER

Luxury Pricing as a Brand Strategy

IN LUXURY, PRICING IS MORE than a number; it's a message. It's like a silent conversation between the brand and its clientele. Done effectively, an excellent pricing strategy validates both the brand's and the buyer's positions in the world.

Pricing decisions are strategic and psychological, making them as critical to brand identity as any other aspect of the brand, such as logo, colors, style, and packaging. However, this strategy is a very delicate dance. The luxury buyer is a savvy customer, so pricing strategy must be thoroughly considered not just for profitability—and certainly not only for the sake of being high-priced—but also for the message it sends.

POSITIONING AND BELONGING

IN LUXURY, PRICING STRATEGY IS about alignment between price and how your customer sees themself in the world. You probably know the idea that if it's not priced high enough, people won't think it's high quality. Pricing therefore is about positioning—it aligns a brand's image and price point with how customers perceive themselves and their sense of belonging. They choose based on where they feel they belong. It's how they see themselves, where they are comfortable, and what they feel they deserve. Luxury buyers are looking for products and services that feel aligned with their own self-image and discerning standards.

It's actually quite arbitrary because pricing is not based on cost of goods but positioning instead. Even within the seemingly narrow field of luxury, there's still a broad range of what a customer feels they can afford or are willing to spend. A luxury brand's pricing strategy then is to understand their customer, how they see themselves in the world, what's comfortable and how much is a stretch, and choose a pricing strategy that speaks to the desired customer.

THE VISUAL SIDE OF PRICING

FOR GOOD REASON, LUXURY BRANDS often adopt "whole pricing"—round numbers, such as $5,000 instead of $4,999. This strategy conveys the message that luxury goods are above the realm of bargains, discounts, or clever pricing tactics that are often seen in the mass market. The rounded pricing style instead of "odd numbers," subtly reinforces that the buyer isn't swayed by cents; they're making a clear and uncluttered decision that mirrors their taste for quality, clarity, and simplicity. Sophisticated shoppers prefer straight-to-the-point pricing with no games or gimmicks.

While luxury pricing should come across as deliberate and not just unsubstantiated high numbers, it should also be a bit vague because this is not a market caught up in dollars and cents. As I like to say, don't nickel and dime them if you don't want to put all the attention on price. Create pricing that doesn't consume attention by being too specific and instead focuses on creating an interaction that elevates the product or service into an exceptional experience and lifestyle choice.

THE IMPORTANCE OF THE "SMART PURCHASE"

WHILE THEY ARE WILLING TO pay for excellence, luxury buyers also appreciate the feeling that they have made a smart choice. This is a delicate line for businesses to navigate, making the buyer feel they've chosen something truly exceptional without crossing into the territory of inflated pricing.

Luxury consumers like a deal, but not in the conventional sense of discounts or promotions. The deal they seek is in finding a brand or item that they believe is worth every penny, offering them value not in savings, but in substance. The luxury buyer is willing to invest at levels that are both comfortable and beyond their comfort levels and also wants to feel assured they have made a smart choice.

One way of accomplishing this is to help them justify the investment. Perhaps an education about the craftsmanship behind the product. Or, the long-term benefit of an investment in a service. Some luxury brands offer tiered pricing or more accessible "entry-level" items (often still high but below the premium offerings) allowing buyers to access the brand without the need for major expenditure. This can create a graduated experience, where buyers feel they're making a smart decision initially, with room to move into higher price brackets in the future.

A sophisticated buyer does not want to feel they made a foolish decision. There's comfort for them in knowing they made a smart choice.

PRICING TRANSPARENCY: TO SHOW OR NOT TO SHOW

IN LUXURY GOODS AND SERVICES, pricing transparency is very nuanced. When prices aren't listed, it can evoke exclusivity and an "If you have to ask, you can't afford it" atmosphere which can be effective. However, a lack of transparency can also deter potential clients, including very qualified luxury buyers by creating uncertainty and fear the product or service might be out of their budget, no matter how high the budget.

To strike a balance, one solution is to offer "starting at" or a price range. It's fine to be somewhat vague but many luxury buyers are comforted by knowing they are at least in the ballpark to ward off any potential embarrassment. A luxury business should be cautious to not inadvertently turn away potential customers because, without pricing transparency, their imaginations may be going wild. Unless your clientele is such that they truly never have to care at any price point, it might be best to offer some pricing guidelines for today's educated, information-seeking luxury buyer.

On one occasion, I was researching restaurants in Paris to host a dinner party for fifteen as part of a retreat for my High Achievers mastermind. There was a substantial budget and I wanted it to be a very special dining experience. The restaurants that were transparent about their prices on their website were far more appealing. Those that weren't made me cautious even though they very well could have been in range of the established budget. Like most luxury buyers, I didn't need to know the exact prices, just that I was at least in range. Imagine then the restaurants that lost out because at least a comforting range of prices were not offered. Sure, I could have called and inquired but like most buyers today, I'm busy, I want to do my research on my own time, find out what I need—especially when there's a several-hour time difference—and move on.

◆ IN THE END...

PRICING NEEDS TO BE STRONGLY considered as part of the brand image and speak the lingo of luxury buyers. It's signaling to luxury buyers that this brand, product line, or service is for them. It's a reflection of their identity, standards, and personal values. By approaching pricing thoughtfully, luxury brands can create a resonance that goes beyond numbers, establishing a relationship based on shared values and appreciation for quality and authenticity.

RALPH LAUREN
Go Big Branding

RALPH LAUREN'S STORY IS A masterclass in branding genius, capturing an American ideal with the bold ambition to "go big." Born in the Bronx, NY, in 1939 to immigrant parents, Lauren transformed his fascination with wealth and elegance into a global lifestyle brand. His success embodies a true American spirit—boundless ambition, relentless vision, and an attitude that says, "Why can't we have it all?"

From the very beginning, Lauren's design style captured an ideal—sprawling estates, rugged ranches, Hamptons beach homes, and the Ivy League charm of the Northeast wealthy. Buying Ralph Lauren wasn't just about owning a product, it was about stepping into a lifestyle that promised success, sophistication, and glamour. Polo anyone?

From his first ties to building an extensive lifestyle brand, Lauren's approach has always been expansive and daring. By 1968, his menswear line redefined classic American style, and by 1971, his women's collection brought the same refinement to a broader audience. But Lauren didn't stop at clothes; he created an entire lifestyle brand. His vision extended to home décor, fragrances, accessories, and even restaurants, all tied together by an idealized American ethos.

With such diversity, it's not easy to stay on brand. What sets Lauren apart is his ability to balance high-end luxury with mass appeal. His couture line stands among the world's finest, while Polo shirts and home furnishings bring his vision to millions. This duality—exclusive yet accessible, thinking without limitation—is distinctly American and undeniably genius.

THE POWER OF LUSCIOUS LANGUAGE

MY BOOK, *LINGO*, IS ABOUT attracting your ideal customers by speaking their language. It's not that I'm a lover of words per se. I'm a lover of the power of influence and energy of words, specifically in luxury marketing and sales. Did you know there isn't a widely recognized single word for someone who is the lover of the *energy* of words? I find this fascinating. Of course, there's logophile for someone who is a lover of the words themselves. The closest I've ever come across as a term for someone who is sensitive to the power of words is a linguistic empath. It's not bad. But the fact that there's a word for a lover of words and not for the energy of words speaks to a world more focused on logic than emotion. Yet, it's fair to say all of us have been affected by just regular ole words said in a different way that carry a very strong energy, good and bad.

I often reference the phrase, "Bless your heart." The words are nice and it can be said as a sincere expression of gratefulness. It can also be said in a way that is equal to "Good thing you're pretty." In my book, *The Self-Employed Life*, I mention how often, when we hear someone say, "You're going to get what you deserve," it sounds like a threat rather than the promise of all good things coming your way.

The energy of the words we use matters every day in every situation. They certainly matter in marketing, branding, and brand messaging. Unlike typical sales and marketing language, which often hinges on utility, the language of luxury must evoke emotions, paint pictures, and shift the energy from negative to positive.

The language of luxury is inherently subtle and persuasive. It avoids overt selling and invites the customer to discover and indulge. Words like "discover," "experience," and "indulge" suggest a journey of personal revelation rather than a commercial transaction. A luxury spa, for example, is not selling treatments but offering a chance to "discover a sanctuary of serenity where every touch is a promise of rejuvenation."

The careful use of words in luxury is about giving items of beauty their fair due and showing acts of service for their full value. Done well, words can make the buyer feel better about their decision. They can offer a respite from the ordinary and evoke an imaginative state, even if just for a moment. So much of what luxury is all about.

Let's look at some examples:

Offers
Ordinary: Discount
Luxury: Upgrade

I often refer to this as reversing the direction. With discounts, you are deducting from the price. With upgrades, you are increasing the value. Luxury buyers favor a positive direction.

Customer Service
Ordinary: Excellent customer service
Luxury: Bespoke customer service tailored to your needs

Excellent customer service is often delivered according to how you've decided you want to give it. Bespoke customer service is about what your customer wants. Do you give the gift you want to give or the gift someone wants to receive?

Quality
Ordinary: High-quality
Luxury: Unwavering commitment to quality and craftsmanship

The key is in the word commitment. It implies that not only is it your intention to provide quality but that you stand by what you deliver. That speaks to integrity and provides comfort to the buyer should anything not live up to expectations.

Guarantee
Ordinary: Satisfaction guaranteed
Luxury: Dedicated to meet and exceed your expectations

There is nothing about the luxury buyer that is happy with being satisfied. They are looking for so much more and want to feel your dedication to meeting what they envision—as if you're an ally on the journey to a destination.

History
Ordinary: In business over twenty years
Luxury: A heritage brand with a legacy of more than two decades

Legacy suggests a long history of very satisfied customers or you wouldn't still be in business. You can "be" in business for as long as you claim. It doesn't mean you pleased anyone. Legacy implies that you have.

Delivery
Ordinary: Fast and reliable service
Luxury: White-glove or concierge delivery

This elevates the delivery from utilitarian to a high level of care.

Now let's consider the energy of words. Both the words you speak and how they might be received as well as the words you say to yourself and the energy you inadvertently create.

I have often joked that marketing words are full of bad energy. For example, target market. If you think of your buyers as a target and they feel targeted, they will back up. If you're looking for a marketing hook, it runs the risk of sounding cheesy. Even calling it a marketing plan sounds conniving.

Some Alternatives for Better Energy
Marketing plan to connection plan
Target market to ideal clientele
Audience to "my people"
Hook to taste of value

This one I love for the luxury clientele:
Often referred to as a discerning clientele, what if we thought of them as a deserving clientele. This is not likely how you will describe your clientele outwardly, but imagine the energy shift within yourself if you thought about your clients as deserving instead of discerning. Perhaps you'd have more patience? Try even harder?

Lastly, I leave you with what may feel like really getting specific but I believe is important. Imagine you've just concluded your exchange with a client, be it a purchase of a luscious face cream or a relaxing massage. You deliver the receipt. So often, people will say, "Here's your receipt for the face cream."

A better way to say that is, "Here's the receipt for your face cream."

What you've done there is make the receipt less personal and the luscious face cream a proud possession. You've put the emphasis on the product as if it's in its pride of place.

Very subtle, shifts the energy, and yes, I am that picky about the energy of words.

◆ IN THE END...

LUXURY BRANDING REQUIRES WORDS THAT evoke sophistication, aspiration, and emotions. The words you choose must carry the energy of how you want to come across, even the unspoken ones. Every word must be chosen with intention, not just to inform but to inspire and resonate. Words that feel misaligned with the luxury buyer, overly promotional, or commonplace can undermine the allure of a luxury experience. Instead, the language should reflect the artistry and care inherent in the brand, subtly inviting buyers to feel the depth, value, and uniqueness of what you offer. With even these few examples, you can start paying much closer to the words you choose—written, spoken, and unspoken—as well as the energy behind the words. Change begins with consciousness. You can start today by consciously choosing the words you use to convey the energy you want to project that will captivate and comfort your luxury clients.

THE HIDDEN KEY TO EVOKING THE EMOTIONS CUSTOMERS WANT TO FEEL

WHEN IT COMES TO LUXURY branding, there's an often-overlooked secret that unlocks everything else. It's not just about a recognizable logo, brand colors, or even the quality of a product or service, though those are all important. It's more than the fact that in luxury, branding is much more expansive and includes everything this highly aware clientele interacts with.

The real magic of luxury branding lies in understanding what the intended customers want to feel and constantly nurturing the brand image and messaging that evokes those precise emotions. This is the hidden key to luxury branding—a reciprocal process that aligns the brand with the ideal buyer's desires, creating a connection so seamless that it becomes almost intuitive. And it's constantly evolving with the client and changing with the times.

It's about designing a brand that resonates so deeply that the ideal buyer doesn't need convincing. They'll step into the world the brand has created because it already feels like their own. This is the alignment that defines a successful luxury brand.

BRAND IDENTITY

EVERY SUCCESSFUL LUXURY BRAND BEGINS with clarity about its identity. What does the brand stand for? What are the core values and philosophies that will shape every touchpoint of the brand? The legacy? This step is foundational. A truly meaningful emotional connection with customers can't be created if the brand's own identity is unclear or inconsistent.

The brand identity is the image and message that's put out into the world. It's the promise of what the brand represents, the lifestyle it embodies, and the value it offers. Is the brand about timeless elegance or bold innovation? Does it reflect a life of understated sophistication or one more showy?

However, clarifying the brand identity is just the first step. Now it must be layered with a deep understanding of the ideal client. This is where most luxury brands fall short. Smaller luxury brands may not do this introspective work to deeply understand the intricacies of their ideal customers. Larger luxury brands may lose touch because of the complex structure of the company from leadership to management, separated by different departments like marketing, all the way to the sales associates on the floor. While iconic luxury brands may have very strong outward-facing brand identity, true luxury branding needs to work its way down all the way to conversations between sales associates and customers. They are in that moment the face of the brand.

UNDERSTAND WHAT YOUR CUSTOMERS WANT TO FEEL

LUXURY BUYERS DON'T JUST BUY products or services—they buy how those products or services make them feel. This isn't about logic or price; it's about emotion. The luxury buyer seeks a specific experience, a feeling that validates their choice and aligns with how they see themselves in the world.

Some luxury buyers want to feel a sense of exclusivity and belonging to an elite circle. Others want to feel they deserve it and feel responsible at the same time as if connected to something meaningful. Some seek simplicity and a reprieve from their busy lives, while others want to feel the thrill of indulgence and treating themselves.

Understanding these emotional drivers requires empathy and observation. It's about stepping into your customers' shoes and asking:

- What emotions drive their decisions?
- What emotions do they want to feel?
- What helps them feel confident and justify their purchase?

This is not a one-size-fits-all exercise. The emotions of the customer and the vibe the brand evokes will each be unique. The key is discovering the overlap between the brand identity and what they want to feel.

CREATE EMOTIONAL ALIGNMENT THROUGH MESSAGING

ONCE YOU KNOW WHAT YOUR customers want to feel, the next step is crafting the messaging and experiences that evoke those emotions. This is where your brand voice, language, and storytelling become powerful tools.

In my book, *LINGO*, I detail the five steps to understanding the secret language of the ideal customer:

- Perspective—understanding their world from walking in their shoes
- Familiarity—understanding what's emotionally and physically comfortable to them
- Style—representing what they want to say about themselves
- Pricing—positioning the brand with how the customer sees themselves in the world
- Words—messaging that speaks their secret language

Your messaging should consistently evoke the emotions your customers are seeking and excellent messaging goes beyond words. It's in the design of the website, the tone of social media, the way staff communicates, and the experience at every touch point. Luxury branding is an entire ecosystem and every element must work together to conjure up the emotions you know the ideal customer wants to feel.

JUSTIFY THE DECISION

A CRITICAL PART OF LUXURY branding is ensuring your customers feel great about their decisions. Buyers in the luxury market often make emotionally driven choices. Even if money is of no concern, they still want those choices to feel justified. They want to feel they made a smart choice. This doesn't mean appealing to logic with a list of product features. It means reinforcing their emotional decision. The best way to accomplish that is by helping them feel the emotions you know they want to feel.

THE RECIPROCITY

WHAT MAKES THIS PROCESS SO powerful is its reciprocity. It's an ever-evolving process of keenly observing the emotions customers want to feel, constantly impacted by what's going on in the world, and realigning a strong brand identity in subtle ways to realign with the customer. In doing so, a luxury brand will naturally continue to attract the right customers while filtering out those who don't resonate with the brand.

When customers see themselves reflected in a luxury brand and feel the emotions they desire, they're not just buying a product, service, or hiring a professional—they're buying into a story, a lifestyle, and an identity. This connection goes beyond the transactional. It's transformative.

♦ IN THE END...

LUXURY BRANDING IS ABOUT CREATING a dynamic relationship between brand identity and customers' emotions. By understanding what your ideal customers want to feel and crafting every element of the brand to evoke those emotions, you unlock the hidden key to luxury branding. This alignment is the difference between a brand that struggles for attention and one that commands attention. In the luxury world, emotions are everything and when this is done right, everything else falls into place.

ELEMENT V

Luxury Customer Relationships

It's more than service; it's the feeling that you've become someone who "gets them" on a personal level—a trusted confidant in their lives.

LUXURY CUSTOMER RELATIONSHIPS
Introduction

THERE ARE COUNTLESS BOOKS ABOUT customer service and customer experience. I'm not even sure why those are considered two different things. Customer service *is* an experience. Furthermore, what if the singular goal of customer service is to build relationships? Or stepped up even further, what I refer to as creating unbreakable bonds. I can assure you, no one in a personal or professional relationship will ever say to you, "You make me feel completely seen, heard, and understood. You surprise and delight me. Therefore, we must break up."

That's an unbreakable bond level of service. Delivering at this level requires listening, observation, creativity, and a desire to go beyond the minimum standards of excellent customer service. Even in conversations about exceptional customer service in the luxury market, it can be a bit cliché: personalized details, attentive staff, pampering, and fulfilling the craziest demands. But true luxury service is something much deeper and more meaningful. It's about building relationships that feel so authentic and personal that clients can't imagine going anywhere else. This kind of service isn't just about catering to someone's needs; it's about knowing them so well that you can surprise them with things they hadn't even thought of. It's staying a few steps ahead, showing up consistently, and making them feel completely seen and valued.

It's often the little things, the unexpected touches, that build this connection. To truly impress in luxury, it's more than the niceties received during the transaction such as the glass of champagne or sparkling water with lime. It's looking beyond the transaction, beyond serving them, to being a curator of memorable experiences.

Like a curator in an art gallery, it takes some creativity to develop exceptional customer service experiences. Exceptional service providers think outside the box and find unexpected ways to make clients feel special. It's about being inspired, tuning into what matters to them, and finding ways to elevate the experience. It's both having systems in place and thinking in the moment. Often, a thoughtful gesture can mean more than an elaborate display of luxury. Once, while staying at The Plaza in New York City, I was in the elevator with my three young kids and a porter from the hotel. Thinking quickly on his feet, he pulled balloons from his pocket and in a short elevator ride, made balloon animals for my kids. And here I am, all these years later, still recalling that moment and spreading the word in a book.

Like the balloon gesture, relationship-building service can also be about what you do for the people your primary customer cares about, rather than just focusing on them directly. As a family portrait photographer, the parents were my clients, and clearly nothing meant more to them than their children. I built such strong relationships with the children, that they would never let their parents hire anyone else! Another client's mother would occasionally visit during the photoshoot and bring her dog along. When I found out that the dog had passed, I sent a message to my client asking her to let her mother know I was sending my condolences. When you extend your care to their family or friends, you're building a level of loyalty that can't be bought. That's what luxury clients appreciate most: when you understand who and what is most important to them. By acknowledging and caring for the people in their lives, you're making it clear that your relationship with them goes beyond just providing a service.

Now, let's talk about consistency. Exceptional luxury service doesn't happen by accident; it's the result of having reliable systems in place that ensure everything happens without a hitch. This may sound overly structured, but systematizing service is what makes it possible to be personal, consistent, and creative. Trust is a high value for an affluent buyer and consistency creates trust; predictability creates comfort. Developing internal systems with room for creativity enables you to deliver at unexpected levels. It allows you to be not only responsive but proactive.

I used to frequently stay at a hotel in Old Quebec City, Canada. After many flawless visits, there was a very minor incident that I brought to the attention of the hotel. Upon our arrival the next time we visited, the moment we checked in, the manager herself appeared from a back room to welcome us back and once again apologize for the ever-so-slight mishap. It was clear this was built into a system so that the next time we checked in, the manager was to be called to the front. The fact this was systematized did not dilute the positive impact. In fact, it made a strong impression that they were that organized. That exchange was followed up with a delivery of freshly made banana bread to our room. They got it right at every step and once again, I am recalling and sharing it with fond memories.

When clients know that each interaction will meet or exceed their expectations, they're more likely to come back. The aim is to make them feel like they're in safe hands every single time, knowing you have their best interests at heart. It's about maintaining that high standard, time and time again, so that your clients never feel like they're taking a risk by choosing you.

In the end, unlike any "normal" or even great level of service, luxury customer service should be about building genuine connections that go beyond any transaction. When you approach it from a place of empathy, care, and consistency, you're not just creating a great experience—you're creating a bond. And in the luxury market, that's what clients value most. It's more than service. It's the feeling that you've become a trusted part of their lives, someone who "gets them" on a personal level. This type of relationship isn't something that can be achieved by being ordinary. Service is the best example that great isn't good enough anymore. To stand out and be memorable, you must be exceptional. It's about showing up authentically, consistently, and with an eye for detail that makes each interaction unforgettable.

This approach to luxury customer service changes how clients perceive the experience. They aren't just looking for excellence; they're looking for a connection, an unspoken understanding that they are cared for, valued, and known. And once that connection is established, it's not easily replaced. That's good business.

UNBREAKABLE BOND LEVEL OF SERVICE

CUSTOMER SERVICE HAS BEEN A perennial topic for businesses for decades. Phrases like "great service" or "outstanding customer experience" have become common in every book and catchphrases in every business. But in the luxury market, great and outstanding aren't enough. If you truly want to stand out, you must set the bar higher. You must aim for what I call an *unbreakable bond level of service*—a service so personalized, intuitive, and understanding that it creates a deep, lasting connection between your brand and your client.

Luxury buyers live in a world where excellence is the baseline. Whether it's products, experiences, or customer service, they've already encountered the best of the best. Traditional methods of impressing customers—like attention to detail or going the extra mile—are expected and no longer enough to truly captivate them.

To break through, you must deliver something exceptional: a level of service that goes beyond fulfilling needs or even exceeding expectations. This means creating a relationship so strong that it feels unbreakable. The secret? Making the client feel completely understood on a surprisingly personal level. When a customer feels *seen* in this way, it builds an emotional connection that transcends the product or service itself.

KNOW THEIR LIVES WHEN THEY ARE NOT IN FRONT OF YOU

WHEN I WAS STARTING OUT, establishing myself as a portrait photographer for affluent families, I often went to the most luxurious stores in Manhattan to observe how they operated and, more importantly, to study the behavior of the customers. On one occasion, I asked for a small item to be gift-wrapped because I understood that stunning packaging was going to be important. After a brief demonstration of gift wrapping which included using a lot of tissue paper and placing the item in a box tied closed with ribbon, the clerk said to me, "Don't use any tape."

When I inquired why I shouldn't use any tape, she went on to explain that before the customer gave the gift, they would likely untie the ribbon, open the box, pull back the tissue paper and make sure the item was in perfect shape. If you used tape, the customer would not be able to do this without destroying the packaging.

Not only was this a great tip, but what impressed me most was this luxury brand didn't just pay attention to the in-store service, but they knew enough about their customer they could imagine the customer's experience outside of the store. In their home. That level of service makes a customer feel completely understood and creates an unbreakable bond with the brand.

THINKING BEYOND THE TRANSACTION

THE LESSON OF THE NO Tape story shaped my own approach to service in my photography business. For instance, our affluent clients often invested significant sums in custom-designed holiday cards featuring portraits of their families or children. These cards weren't just stationery—they were a statement, a reflection of their lifestyle, sent to the most important people in their lives.

Knowing this, we didn't just deliver the cards. We role-played their experience after receiving them. For example, our clients would never dream of addressing these elegant envelopes with an ordinary black pen. They'd want a pen that perfectly matched the ink color of the return address—whether it was holiday red, green, or blue. Not having a matching pen on hand, they, or someone on their staff, would have spent hours visiting local stationery shops searching for the perfect pen.

So, we included the pen. One pen for every 100 cards. It was a thoughtful but inexpensive gesture that saved them time and effort. The first time clients discovered the pen, their reaction was as if we had gifted them fine jewelry. Afterward, it became something they expected—and eagerly looked for—with every order.

This wasn't just attention to detail; it was a demonstration that we understood their lives, their priorities, and their preferences. That simple pen built trust and loyalty in a way no marketing campaign ever could.

THE ART OF ROLE-PLAYING YOUR CLIENT'S LIFE

CREATING AN UNBREAKABLE BOND STARTS with stepping into your client's shoes. How will they experience your product or service beyond the point of sale? What challenges or needs might arise? How can you anticipate these and solve them before they even realize they exist?

In the luxury market, it's not enough to provide exceptional service during the transaction. The magic happens when you extend your thoughtfulness into the client's life beyond that moment. This requires empathy, imagination, and a commitment to understanding your client's world deeply.

Ask yourself:

- What are my clients' daily routines and preferences?
- How does the product or service I provide show up in their lives at other times?
- How can I add value to their experience beyond the immediate interaction?

When you take the time to role-play their lives—thinking through every touchpoint—you gain the insights needed to deliver service that feels almost psychic. And when clients feel that you "just get them," you've achieved a level of connection that's unbreakable.

CONSISTENCY BUILDS DEVOTION

ONCE YOU'VE CREATED THIS BOND, maintaining it requires consistency. The details that initially wowed your client—whether it's the perfect pen, thoughtful gift wrapping, or personalized follow-up—must become a hallmark of your brand. Luxury buyers notice the smallest lapses in service. If by chance we forgot to include the pen with holiday cards, believe me, clients would let us know. On more than one occasion I was driving pens to client's homes. It's worth it though because if these special gestures feel inconsistent or disingenuous, the bond weakens.

When you deliver this level of care consistently, you transform customer loyalty into something much deeper: *devotion*. This devotion isn't just about liking your product or service; it's about an emotional alignment with your brand. Clients feel they can rely on you—not just to meet their needs, but to make their lives better in meaningful ways.

♦ IN THE END...

CREATING AN UNBREAKABLE BOND LEVEL of service isn't just about building loyalty. It's about transforming the relationship between your brand and your clients into something more meaningful. Like a partnership built on mutual understanding and trust. When clients feel seen, heard, and valued in this way, they don't just become repeat customers; they become lifelong advocates for your brand.

In the luxury market, where expectations are sky-high, this level of service is the ultimate differentiator. It's the key to standing out, building trust, and ensuring your clients never even think about going elsewhere. After all, when someone truly understands you, why would you ever want to leave?

CHÂTEAU FRONTENAC
Orchestrated Customer Service

CHÂTEAU FRONTENAC IN OLD QUEBEC City is not only one of the most photographed hotels in the world but also a masterclass in *hospitality with heart*, excelling in customer service through a deep focus on personalized experiences and attention to detail. One of its most fascinating stories involves its *romantic concierge services*, which have earned it a reputation as a destination for love stories.

In one memorable instance, a guest planning to propose sought help from the Château Frontenac staff. What followed was a carefully orchestrated event that showcased the hotel's ability to go above and beyond. The team arranged for a private horse-drawn carriage ride through the cobblestone streets of Old Quebec, followed by a candlelit dinner in a secluded part of the hotel, overlooking the St. Lawrence River. The proposal was timed perfectly to coincide with a surprise fireworks display, arranged by the hotel through its local connections. Every detail, down to the couple's favorite flowers and a personalized playlist, was meticulously planned.

Beyond romantic gestures, the hotel builds lasting relationships by engaging with guests before, during, and after their stay. They remember anniversaries, preferences, and even small details, ensuring returning guests feel as if they're coming home.

These stories exemplify how Château Frontenac transforms stays into lifelong memories. Such orchestrated customer service doesn't happen by chance. It's the result of having systems in place that enable the freedom to respond to the moment in creative ways.

WHY "KNOW, LIKE, AND TRUST" IS TOO LOW OF A BAR AND WHAT TO DO ABOUT IT

FOR YEARS, THE BUSINESS WORLD has embraced the mantra of "know, like, and trust" as the cornerstone of effective marketing and customer relationships. And while this may suffice in many industries, it falls far short in the luxury market. Serving a sophisticated buyer with high expectations requires transcending these basic principles to create meaningful connections, foster brand devotion, and build intimate trust. Luxury buyers demand a relationship with a brand that is anything but ordinary. They seek experiences and relationships that resonate with their identity, aspirations, and values—something far deeper than simply knowing, liking, or trusting a provider.

Let's explore why this is true and what it takes to create meaningful engagement with the luxury audience.

DEEPER RELATIONSHIPS

IN THE LUXURY MARKET, RELATIONSHIPS don't just rely on excellent service or attentiveness—they thrive on emotional connection. For luxury buyers, it's not enough for a brand to listen to their needs or fulfill their requests. They seek a partner, a confidant, and an ally in achieving their goals, whether it's finding the perfect product, designing a special experience, or creating a vision that reflects their taste and aspirations.

At its core, this is about making the buyer feel understood on an intimate level. It's not just about "knowing" them in the transactional sense, like memorizing their preferences or past purchases. It's about knowing what they need, often before they express it themselves. This requires empathy, attentiveness, listening, and intuition.

A luxury client isn't simply shopping for an item or service; they are often validating a piece of their identity. When you become their ally in that journey, you help them discover what aligns with their sense of self. It's not just about closing a sale—it's about building a bridge of mutual understanding that stands the test of time.

BRAND DEVOTION

LUXURY BUYERS ALIGN THEMSELVES WITH a brand that reflects their identity. The choices they make in the luxury market are deeply tied to how they see themselves in the world. A luxury brand must understand this and deliver not just quality and craftsmanship but an emotional resonance that reinforces the buyer's self-image.

What makes a buyer devote themselves to a brand? It's not just the quality and promise of excellence. It's the feeling that the brand shares their values, speaks their lingo, and enhances their personal narrative. For many luxury buyers, this connection is grounded in the brand's heritage, story, and brand image. The brand becomes more than a provider of goods or services—it becomes a statement of taste and an extension of the buyer's personality.

True brand devotion requires that the buyer feels seen and understood. This goes beyond simply "liking" a brand. True devotion is when the buyer experiences the brand as a shared expression of their own values and style.

INTIMATE TRUST

ONE OF THE MOST DISTINCTIVE aspects of serving the luxury buyer is the level of trust they place in their chosen providers. But this isn't just ordinary trust—it's intimate trust. Luxury buyers often seek providers who can step into their world with discretion, care, and an unwavering commitment to their best interests.

This kind of trust is deeply personal. As someone who spent forty years as a family photographer, I've had the privilege of building such relationships. I often describe my experience in the luxury market by saying, "I don't just know this market, I was in their closets for forty years." And I mean that literally—I was there, helping clients decide how they wanted to look, how they wanted to be perceived, what was flattering and what was not, and even navigating family dynamics through the lens of a portrait session. These moments required more than professionalism. They demanded empathy, attentiveness, and a genuine desire to serve.

Intimate trust is built through active listening, authenticity, and a consistent demonstration of putting the buyer's needs first. Luxury buyers often carry significant responsibilities and pressures as they enjoy their privileges. They don't want to feel catered to in a superficial way; they want to know that their provider understands their unique situation and is working sincerely on their behalf.

When this level of trust is achieved, the buyer feels safe leaning on the provider's expertise. They no longer feel the need to micromanage or second-guess decisions. Instead, they can enjoy the experience, confident that their provider has their best interests at heart. This level of trust isn't about power or authority—it's about creating a partnership where the buyer feels genuinely cared for and understood.

◆ IN THE END...

THE TRADITIONAL "KNOW, LIKE, AND trust" framework is a starting point, but it's far too low of a bar for the luxury market. In this space, excellence isn't just about meeting expectations—it's about creating relationships, experiences, and connections that far surpass them. Luxury buyers expect to feel valued, understood, and celebrated at every turn.

Deeper relationships, brand devotion, and intimate trust aren't just strategies—they're the hallmark of a successful luxury brand. It requires thoughtfulness, intention, and a willingness to go beyond the ordinary. Ultimately, serving the luxury buyer is about making them feel extraordinary—not just through the products or services provided, but through the relationship you cultivate with them. When done well, these relationships create an authentic sense of connection and loyalty that benefits both buyer and brand. Luxury isn't just about delivering something exceptional; it's about building something exceptional together.

For businesses looking to succeed in the luxury space, don't settle for "know, like, and trust." Aim higher. Strive to create the kind of connection that leaves a lasting impression, the kind of trust that feels deeply personal, and the kind of devotion that makes your brand unforgettable. Because in the luxury market, anything less than exceptional simply won't do.

CROSS-INNOVATION
Creating Exceptional Customer Service

EXCEPTIONAL CUSTOMER SERVICE IS OFTEN the pride of luxury businesses. However, by definition, to be exceptional means to be "unusual or not typical." Yet often, customer service becomes standardized and expected. How then might a luxury brand truly stand out and differentiate? With cross-innovation perhaps.

When I interviewed Julie Cottineau, author of *Twist: How Fresh Perspectives Build Breakthrough Brands* for my podcast, she shared the origin story for the book. She explained that while waiting to board a plane, she looked out at the tarmac and saw a plane with the McDonald's logo on it. She wondered, "When did McDonald's get into the airline business?" She then realized the highly recognizable logo was a reflection from inside the gate that happened to land perfectly on the plane. But it got her wheels turning. What would it look like if McDonald's was an airline?

This type of inquiry is the foundation for cross-innovation and can spur tremendous creativity to develop exceptional customer service ideas beyond the ordinary. Imagining the intersection of two wildly different ideas, such as McDonald's and an airline, with a willingness to look way outside the box of their current industry and marketplace, cross-innovation can encourage luxury brands to seek inspiration for exceptional customer service that goes beyond the expected.

LEARNING FROM LUXURY

THE RITZ-CARLTON IS OFTEN CITED as the pinnacle of luxury service, but what makes its approach exceptional? The company is known for its "service recovery" approach, where any employee is empowered to spend up to $2,000 to resolve a guest issue without management approval. Such an idea as this demonstrates absolute commitment to customer satisfaction.

Luxury service providers can borrow this idea of employee empowerment and customer service and adapt it to their own brands. Imagine if high-end retailers could offer sales associates the opportunity to make on-the-spot decisions to replace damaged goods, upgrade services, or offer complimentary perks when needed. Just imagine how that would deescalate numerous service pain points.

Another example of best-in-class service is NetJets, a private jet company that sells fractional ownership shares in private business jets. They offer "anticipatory service," where very personal preferences are logged so seamlessly that returning clients feel every flight is tailored precisely to their tastes. The idea of anticipatory service and highly detailed personal preferences profiles can be applied to many businesses. For example, a luxury spa might include in personalized profile for each guest: their preferred scents, tea choices, or even favorite post-treatment playlists. Or know which guests prefer Monkfruit sweetener over sugar for dietary reasons.

Time is another welcomed customer service luxury. Time can be both generously given and thoughtfully saved, and each can feel like the ultimate in luxury. When a client feels that they have someone's unlimited time—whether it's a sales associate patiently guiding them through their choices, unhurried concierge service, or a service provider devoted to meticulous details without a sense of rush—it creates a deep sense of care.

Conversely, luxury can also be found in the saving of time. For individuals whose lives are filled with demands, the ability to bypass unnecessary steps, have needs anticipated before they arise, or enjoy seamless efficiency becomes a welcomed gift. A brand that is known to excel at both the giving of time and efficient service is the world's largest cashmere manufacturer, Loro Piana. A visit to their store is about savoring the moment—feeling the cashmere, learning about the craftsmanship, and always engaging in meaningful dialogue with staff who never seem to be in a hurry.

At the same time, Loro Piana is known for their VIP services which anticipate needs, remove friction, and create a seamless experience that respects the client's busy life.

Brands that have mastered this time duality, knowing when to create space for luxurious time experience and when to offer time-saving precision, can be found in many luxury brands and expand current customer service offerings.

Bulgari Hotels, an extension of the iconic luxury jewelry brand, goes beyond traditional amenities to create hyper-personalized experiences. Guests are offered a "pillow menu," where they can select from various options to suit their preferred sleeping style. While this isn't unheard of in luxury hospitality, Bulgari takes it further with a signature touch. They pair the pillow selection with a curated fragrance that complements the sleep experience. This attention to multisensory detail enhances relaxation while reinforcing the brand's luxurious identity.

Luxury businesses could adapt this idea by considering the multisensory experience, not only during the transaction but also in packaging and delivery. Touch, smell, and sound, all create a powerful experience for the customer. This applies also to knowing when customers may have sensitivities to scents and smells and avoiding them to create best-in-class service.

INSPIRATION BEYOND LUXURY

WHILE IT'S TEMPTING TO FOCUS solely on the luxury market for inspiration, some of the most innovative customer service ideas come from unexpected places. One of my most effective service strategies was inspired by Starbucks. When they introduced the gift card—originally more about convenience for the buyer and possibly an element of being cool than it was about gift-giving—I saw the potential to apply the same principle of pre-paying and "being in the know" to my high-end photography business. By offering clients the ability to pre-pay for their portrait session with the introduction of my Priority Client Pre-Pay Offer, I was able to provide them with priority scheduling, a privilege they appreciated, as well as being part of a select group of clients. When open to cross-innovation, you can find inspiration even in a cup of coffee for a luxury business.

Of course, companies like Apple and Amazon are well known for having set high standards for customer service. Apple set a new standard for clever packaging design and Amazon of course has completely redefined the meaning of speed and convenience. Sure, luxury buyers want quality. Customers still want quality—but they want quality faster. If a business holds steadfast to the old adage that quality takes time, in today's world, it may cause a customer to seek a different service provider that can offer both quality and speed.

Many NYC Broadway productions have embraced cross-innovation by creating immersive experiences while also putting on a show in the traditional stage format. I've attended numerous Broadway shows in recent years that completely transformed theaters into clubs and speakeasies, where the performance actually begins an hour before the show with entertainers canvasing the venue and engaging with attendees as soon as they arrive through the door. These productions transport their guests into another world, engaging their senses and emotions at every turn well before the traditional stage performance even begins.

Similarly, luxury brands can learn to focus on not just what they sell and the transaction experience—the main stage performance—but also on the atmosphere they create and all the moments before and after the primary act of service.

Luxury brands would serve themselves well to see new standards set by non-luxury brands as the minimum bar which they now must exceed if they want to maintain their luxury status.

TIPS TO INSPIRE CROSS-INNOVATION

- **Observe industries that seem unrelated**
  Look outside your industry for creative ideas and inspiration. What makes their service stand out? What clever ideas are they implementing?

- **Focus on eliminating friction**
  What frustrations do your customers face, and how do other industries solve similar problems? How might you reduce friction in your business?

- **Combine elements**
  Sometimes the best ideas come from blending what appear to be completely different concepts, like fast food and an airline. What can you learn from a completely opposite industry?

◆ IN THE END...

THE LUXURY MARKET THRIVES ON exceeding expectations. Yet, it's easy to become ordinary, even if the standard is high, by relying on tried-and-true methods of customer service. Cross-innovation breathes fresh life into service strategies by encouraging businesses to think outside of the box.

Luxury clients expect not only excellence but also uniqueness. Cross-innovation isn't just a creative exercise, it's a competitive advantage. So, look around. The next big idea for your luxury business might be hiding in plain sight.

FRETTE

Knowing What's Going on in the Bedroom

FRETTE, THE ITALIAN LUXURY LINEN brand, distinguishes itself by blending personalized service with a deep understanding of each client's lifestyle, creating unparalleled customer relationships. Their approach isn't just about selling linens—it's about raising the level of importance of their products and building a relationship exclusively tailored to each customer.

What sets Frette apart is their white-glove service, particularly for high-end clients such as luxury hotels, yachts, and private residences. Frette doesn't just sell bedding; they offer a bedroom design consultation, working directly with clients to craft cohesive and personalized settings. This includes advising on color schemes, thread counts, and even custom embroidery, ensuring every detail aligns with the client's taste and space.

Frette excels in anticipating customer needs, often reaching out proactively with seasonal suggestions and for special occasions. For instance, they might suggest lightweight linens for summer or cleverly designed gift sets for holiday family gatherings, turning routine purchases into thoughtful moments.

Their VIP clients enjoy even more exclusive perks, such as private shopping appointments, access to limited-edition collections, and invitations to brand events at flagship stores or luxury venues. These experiences create a sense of community and belonging, reinforcing loyalty and brand connection.

Frette's mastery lies in their ability to raise the bar on what might otherwise be an ordinary household purchase. By offering tailored solutions and immersive experiences, they position themselves not just as a provider of luxury linens but as partners in the art of living beautifully.

STAYING A STEP AHEAD
Anticipation over Details

OTHER THAN QUALITY, IF YOU asked most people what stands out as a hallmark of luxury goods and services, most people would say attention to detail. While still important, in today's competitive market, paying attention to detail alone may no longer be enough to impress.

Today's luxury buyers are sophisticated, discerning, and expect more on every level. They want to work with a brand that also anticipates their needs and feels one step ahead. This means shifting focus from not only impressing with details but also deeply understanding and anticipating the nuanced needs of their clientele.

Here's why and how luxury goods and service businesses should prioritize anticipation over details to captivate and keep their customers.

HARD TO IMPRESS THE EXPERIENCED BUYER

FOR THE LUXURY BUYER, THERE'S hardly any exceptional experience or level of customer service they have not experienced. When you're accustomed to the best, where do you go from there?

Over my many decades as a family portrait photographer for affluent families, I would often have wedding photographers wanting to collaborate with me since that was not a service I offered. They imagined being a wedding photographer for a wealthy clientele would be a dream come true. I would explain that while a very special day and certainly a glorious celebration of their union, wedding days among the wealthy are not the biggest days of their lives. It's likely not the first time a bride wore a white dress or gown—she may have been a debutante—and it's certainly not their first ride in a limo.

So, where do you go when the people you serve have already experienced the best of the best? You stay a step ahead and anticipate their needs before they need to ask. It's attention to detail at a whole other level.

To impress the unimpressible requires businesses to do more than provide an attention to detail. They expect that. Instead, develop a deep understanding of customers' lifestyles, preferences, and behaviors and anticipate their needs. Be a step ahead. That will impress.

Here are some ideas:

- **Systemized Individualization**

    While systemization may initially feel like the antithesis of individualization, done right, proper systems can help a business stay a step ahead and actually make customers feel like they are the one and only, even at scale.

    A simple way is to ask the right questions upfront that will provide insights to stay a step ahead later for example. You could find out upfront how your client wants to be communicated with: Text, WhatsApp, phone call, email, etc. With so many communication channels, it's not up to the business to decide how they want to do business but to systematically find out what the preference is for each individual client.

    Data integration across locations or even devices can enable a business to have what they need on hand to provide the customer with the information or support they need at a moment's notice or preemptively. With cloud-based services, gone are the excuses that "It's on my laptop," or "I'll let you know when I get back to the office." Systems that enable a business to respond quickly from anywhere make the customer feel they are important.

    Standardized personalization can seem like a contradictory term, but once again, it's a case of creating a system to personalize preferences in order to stay a step or two ahead of their requests. For instance, The Peninsula Hotels chain operates an advanced guest preference system across their global properties. Once a guest stays at one Peninsula property, their preferences are meticulously recorded—everything from pillow type, room temperature, minibar preferences, preferred newspaper, and even how they take their coffee in the morning. This information is stored in a centralized system accessible to staff across all Peninsula locations worldwide. When the guest books a stay at any other Peninsula hotel, these preferences are automatically applied, and staff are briefed ahead of their arrival.

Done exceptionally well, these systems feel invisible to the customer who in the end, feels like the one and only.

- **Leveraging Technology**

    I've been saying for many years that technology can be used to create a less personal experience or a more personal experience. The choice will be up to the business and how they handle the available technology.

    For instance, whereas AI-powered chatbots can seem impersonal, done well and with transparency that it is in fact a bot, they can provide a client with immediate and customized responses to customer inquiries, saving the client a lot of time. Like, "Where is my package?" There also must be a quick exit out of the bot and into contact with a person if needed and this is where many brands are failing right now.

    We also should not assume everyone hates cookies and being tracked online. I, for one, am a fan of the assistance. If machine learning algorithms can make solid recommendations based on individual browsing and purchase history, that could be a huge time and energy saver. Only if done well, of course. This proactive approach ensures that the customer feels catered to at every touchpoint.

Predictive analytics and artificial intelligence can also play a crucial role in anticipating customer needs. These tools allow brands to analyze vast amounts of data to predict future behaviors and trends. By understanding what customers are likely to want before they even realize it themselves, brands can create individualized marketing campaigns and develop new products and services that match the anticipated needs of their customers.

- **Proactive Customer Service**

   Exceptional customer service is a hallmark of luxury brands, but to truly anticipate customer needs, brands must be proactive rather than reactive. This means reaching out to customers before they encounter issues or have to make requests. Proactive customer service also involves following up after purchase to ensure satisfaction and address any potential concerns. This level of attentiveness demonstrates that the brand cares about the customer's experience and is committed to anticipating their needs.

◆ IN THE END...

IN TODAY'S COMPETITIVE LUXURY MARKET, attention to detail is no longer enough to captivate sophisticated buyers who have experienced the best. Luxury brands must go beyond by anticipating client needs and staying a step ahead. This requires a deep understanding of customers' lives, systemized individualization, leveraging technology for personalized experiences, and proactive customer service that addresses concerns before they arise. By prioritizing anticipation over detail, luxury businesses can create exceptional, forward-thinking experiences that keep their discerning clientele engaged and loyal.

THE ART OF FOLLOW-THROUGH
Finding the Perfect Balance

FOLLOW-THROUGH AS A CUSTOMER SERVICE touchpoint has become very complex and an essential skill to develop. In the true spirit of service, follow-through is not just about post-sale checking in, but also includes interaction well before the transaction. The bottom line is, it's no longer enough to deliver a great product or service. How you engage with your clients before and after the transaction often defines their long-term perception of a luxury brand. Done well, effective engagement builds trust, enhances loyalty, and strengthens relationships. Done poorly, it risks annoying clients, making them feel unimportant, or even alienating them.

It's not just about staying top of mind; it's an act of service. When done right, it shows clients you care about their satisfaction and success. It demonstrates that your relationship with them isn't purely transactional but also deeply valued.

If a client feels genuinely valued, they are far more likely to return, recommend you to others, and engage with your business at a deeper level. Conversely, if follow-up efforts feel insincere or excessive, it can ruin a previously great relationship.

Navigating the fine line between meaningful communication and overstepping boundaries requires finesse, sensitivity, and a deep understanding of individual client preferences.

KNOWING WHEN IT'S TOO MUCH

THE CHALLENGE WITH FOLLOW-THROUGH LIES in determining the right frequency and tone. Bombarding clients with upsell emails, product recommendations, or generic marketing messages can quickly cross the line into annoyance. Especially when communication has been inconsistent. Pay attention to how clients respond to follow-up efforts. A lack of engagement with emails, texts, or calls is a sign to step back. Conversely, clients who respond positively or engage in meaningful ways may welcome further communication.

The depth of the relationship also matters a great deal. Randomly receiving a text when it was a very transactional experience can feel invasive. Yet if the exchange was meaningful or the relationship ongoing, it can be welcomed. Carefully consider how the customer might evaluate the depth of your relationship when thinking about frequency of communication, keeping in mind you are likely one small part of their complex lives.

You could also consider a "permission-based" approach by asking upfront how often they'd like to hear from you or if they're open to future recommendations. This creates clarity and avoids assumptions. Following up on a luxury purchase or service with a thoughtful handwritten note or sincere message can feel warm and genuine. Following it up with three consecutive phone calls can feel excessive and pushy.

On the other hand, failing to follow up adequately can leave clients feeling undervalued or neglected. The key is striking a balance that makes them feel seen without overwhelming them.

Certainly, if a customer raises an issue, it's crucial to resolve it. Not doing so can leave them wondering if their feedback was even taken seriously.

THE DELICATE BALANCE OF REMINDERS

Reminders, whether for upcoming appointments or future service opportunities, can be incredibly helpful, or incredibly frustrating, depending on how they're handled. Some clients appreciate a gentle nudge, as it helps them stay organized and feel cared for. Others, however, may view repeated reminders as unnecessary or even intrusive, especially if they're good about managing their commitments.

Try to strike a balance by offering clients the choice of how they'd like to receive reminders, if they want them at all. We know the rate of people forgetting appointments has greatly increased over the years which is why reminders have become so popular. But on the other hand, some people are far more organized than others and don't need reminders at all. Perhaps the best you can do is keep the tone very light, brief, and service-oriented, such as, "Just a quick note to remind you of your appointment this Friday at 2 PM" or "I look forward to seeing you Friday at 2 PM. I'll be there with bells on and an extra stash of chocolate." Keep the tone service-oriented, even including links or a contact number. The goal is for reminders to feel like you are trying to make their life easier and less like you doubt their ability to be responsible.

FOLLOWING UP WITH PROSPECTIVE CLIENTS

ENGAGING WITH A POTENTIAL CLIENT requires even more delicacy. The goal is to express your commitment and interest without veering into pushiness. Sincerity is rooted in authentic care, while pushiness is self-serving. Prospective clients can sense the difference. Stay focused on their needs and what they can gain. Don't follow up with, "Have you made a decision yet?" Place the focus on seeing what they are thinking. Or better yet, offer insights and value while they are still considering your offer.

The energy by which you follow up will likely have everything to do with the result you get. Someone can easily come across as pushy yet someone else, perhaps even more pushy, can come across as being committed to the customer's well-being if that's truly what they hold in their hearts.

- **Make It Natural**

  The best way to manage follow-throughs is to make it natural to who you are. I'll bet you have a natural sense how often you should be in touch with a parent or a good friend. You know how to be in touch often enough and also how upset they might be if they don't hear from you often enough. In many ways, our client relationships are the same.

- **Surprise and Delight**
  Send a small, thoughtful gesture related to their purchase or the time spent together. I would often send candid cell phone photos from a photo session, shortly after, as a preview or coming attraction and to stay close to the client, letting them know their photos would be coming soon.

- **Create Value Beyond the Sale**
  Offer something of value that has no strings attached. Share an insightful article, an event invitation, or a "thought of you" type of message. I often share words of wisdom to coaching clients and prospective clients.

◆ IN THE END...

REMEMBER, WHAT MAKES FOLLOW-THROUGH SO challenging is it's not a one-size-fits-all solution. You have to figure out how to systemize follow-through for consistent and effective customer service and also recognize that every client is unique, and what works for one may not work for another. This paradox is exactly what makes it complex and an opportunity to be exceptional. Your ability to read cues, understand preferences, and customize your approach is what separates meaningful follow-through from mediocre follow-up.

When done with care and intention, follow-through becomes a relationship-building art form that keeps your clients coming back and sets you apart from everyone else.

ELEMENT VI

Luxury Sales

The care and attention given to every detail of the sales process—whether it's the story behind a product, the service provided, or the experience of choosing—all contribute to an experience that feels deeply immersive and meaningful.

LUXURY SALES
Introduction

HERE WE ARE, SHARING ABOUT sales in the last Element of a book about selling to the rich. This might seem counterintuitive. But as explained in Who You're Meant to Serve, the real way to *sell to the rich* is to grasp all the other concepts first because selling in the traditional sense, without rethinking our perspectives, our mindsets, the unique behaviors of the luxury buyer, and all the ways we interact with them, is exactly what will repel them. Selling to the rich shouldn't feel like traditional selling at all. It certainly didn't to me. It felt like something far more connective—an exchange that was deeply bonding, deeply human, and mutually rewarding.

Sure, I could offer some trite phrases like selling is service or selling is about moving people—both of which are true. However, selling to the rich—this elusive and exceptional clientele—can be far more meaningful than that. Whether it's a long-standing client relationship or a one-time exchange, the potential exists for sales to be so much more.

Selling to affluent buyers defies many of the stereotypes people often associate with luxury sales. For those who have never been immersed in this world, it's easy to imagine high-maintenance clients, impersonal transactions, or the seller catering to the buyer's every whim. Yet in my experience, that couldn't be further from the truth. Selling in the luxury market doesn't just feel different—it is different.

Selling to the luxury market goes beyond a relationship—it's a partnership. It's a one-of-a-kind collaboration in which you are a key part of their story in achieving their lifestyle and identity. At the heart of it is a shared recognition of value. The transaction is a technicality. Luxury buyers desire and respect expertise, quality, and care, and they engage deeply when they see these qualities. The buyer feels uplifted by the attention and quality being offered, while the seller feels honored to provide something meaningful. This is the dynamic that creates a collaboration, not a transaction. And that nuance is why this Element must come last in this book. It's hard to grasp, easy to miss, but is the very cornerstone of why selling is not really selling. And rich is not about finances. Still, we'll use the term luxury sales to be straightforward on the seller's side.

As I considered why luxury sales have always felt different to me, both as a seller for forty-plus years and a frequent consumer of luxury brands, what stands out in these exchanges are the moments of shared humanity. Despite the elevated experience of luxury, these moments remind us that everyone is human, regardless of wealth or status. A shared laugh, a personal story, or a simple but heartfelt gesture can transform the interaction. These small, authentic moments often leave the deepest impressions. The value is on the collaboration of the moment, of the story. For luxury buyers, who are frequently engaged in relationships that are far more surface-level, such genuine moments feel refreshing and rare. I have felt this strongly as both the service provider and the customer.

Empathy plays a key role in making these interactions meaningful. Affluent clients, perhaps more than many realize, appreciate service that is straightforward and unpretentious. Their lives, while privileged, are often complex and full of pressure. Sales experiences with care, understanding, and authenticity create an atmosphere where intimacy can flourish.

When a seller takes the time to see beyond the financial aspect and understands their customers' unique desires, needs, and stories, the experience becomes incredibly personal. This sense of being seen creates

a connection that's deeper than the encounter itself. It makes the buyer feel valued for who they are, not just for what they can afford. Taking time is also key. Time often works differently in luxury sales. The pace is in many cases slower and more intentional, as it's likely not a small decision. Sellers and buyers alike are fully present, focused entirely on the interaction. These moments feel timeless as if the outside world has paused. The care and attention given to every detail, whether it's the story behind a product, the service provided, or the process of choosing, all contribute to a sales experience that feels deeply immersive and meaningful.

The mutual respect between seller and buyer creates a sense of co-creation that defines the best luxury sales experiences. Both buyer and seller contribute something and are committed to creating value. The buyer brings their vision, personality, and aspirations, while the seller provides expertise, guidance, and care. The result feels more like art crafted between two people than business.

The best sales environments create an alignment that is rare in life but deeply satisfying when it occurs. The connection with a luxury buyer often feels like being perfectly in tune with someone, kind of like a dance where you anticipate their needs and they trust your expertise. This harmony makes the interaction not just memorable but transformative, leaving both parties with a sense of fulfillment that goes beyond the sale.

Perhaps the most extraordinary aspect of selling in the luxury market is the way these moments transcend the ordinary sales environment. When doing business is about creating life-transforming moments, the interaction isn't just about fulfilling a need, it's about creating an experience that feels elevated and memorable. Both buyer and seller walk away changed, having shared an experience.

Luxury isn't about things. It's about the stories, emotions, and identities wrapped up in those things. Affluent buyers are not always seeking to be impressed or indulged. They are often looking for someone to meet them where they are, to co-create something extraordinary, and to make them feel valued as individuals.

Selling in the luxury market offers sellers a chance to respond to a call for greatness and build relationships that last long after the transaction is complete. It's not just about delivering a product or service, it's about creating a shared experience that resonates on a deeper level. It's what can make the sales process profoundly fulfilling. Luxury sales are a reminder that, at their best, business transactions can be as much about people and life as they are about offerings—and that's what makes them so uniquely meaningful.

HOW TO BE CHOSEN BY CLIENTS WITH UNLIMITED CHOICES

WHAT'S OFTEN SAID TO BE one of the biggest challenges in marketing today that I believe is one of the greatest excuses, is that consumers don't have an attention span. It's not that people don't have attention, it's that there are so many things vying for attention. In the luxury market, where the clientele is not often constrained by cost, this challenge is magnified. To stand out, businesses must go beyond being excellent in their field. They must strive to be the most compelling option among all possible choices.

THE ATTENTION CHALLENGE

WHILE MARKETERS AND BUSINESS OWNERS can claim people don't have attention any longer, Netflix has proven that to not be true. I propose that the real truth is people are selective about where they direct their valuable time and focus, given the overwhelming number of options vying for attention. This is especially true for luxury buyers, who typically have the resources to explore a seemingly unlimited set of possibilities. And if we're brutally honest, many brands simply aren't saying anything attention-worthy.

Every time the luxury world gasps at the potential downfall of what had been a leading luxury brand, I wonder what the surprise is. In almost all cases, the brand hadn't done anything for years to stay innovative, relevant, and attention worthy. Tired branding and limited evolution in a world of luxury buyers with massive decision potential is a fatal position. I like to suggest to marketing professionals to imagine they have to pass the Netflix test. Imagine your ideal customer lounging at home with a laptop propped in front of them while fully engaged in the latest and hottest Netflix series. Let's say an ad for your brand comes across their laptop screen. Is it good enough to capture their attention? To distract them from Netflix? Maybe to turn to the person beside them and say, "Check this out." That's passing the Netflix test. That's being attention-worthy. The bar for gaining attention is that high.

BEYOND QUALITY

IN THE LUXURY MARKET, QUALITY, performance, and experience are table stakes—they're expected, not differentiators. They also all come post-decision to buy or hire you. But how do you get chosen in the first place? The promise must feel so significant that it stands out in the buyer's mind as being life-transforming.

Does a pledge of transformation sound too lofty for some purchases? Perhaps. But in a world of nearly infinite options, the luxury buyer needs to feel that their decision carries significant meaning.

Interior designer Nate Berkus masterfully positions his design work as life-transforming by shifting the focus from aesthetics to emotion. Rather than selling furniture arrangements or color palettes, Nate sells how it feels to live in the space. The warmth of a sunlit breakfast nook, a cherished family heirloom displayed with care, or the comfort of a room that feels like a sanctuary. Through emotionally resonant messaging like, *"A home should feel like a hug, not a showroom,"* he invites clients to envision daily moments and future memories in their redesigned spaces. By weaving storytelling and a deep understanding of his clients' lives into his messaging, Nate doesn't just promise beautiful rooms—he promises a home where life feels better, richer, and more soulful.

Luxury purchases often fulfill deeper emotional needs, such as legacy, pride, or indulgence. To stand out among unlimited choices, brands must tap into these emotional triggers. It's not just about what the product is, it's about what it represents and how it makes the buyer feel.

NOT APPLES TO APPLES

ONE OF THE UNIQUE CHALLENGES in the luxury market is that your luxury buyer isn't just deciding between two high-end brands in the same category. They're comparing your offering to entirely different experiences and investments. The key is to help the buyer reframe their perspective and see your offering as the best among all their choices. This doesn't mean dismissing other options but rather positioning your product or service as the most rewarding choice among them.

As a family portrait photographer, I never worried about the so-called competition of other photographers. Quite honestly, in most cases, I was out of their league with a price point most would only dream of. I was concerned about all the other places my clients could spend a comparable amount of money. On jewelry, a weekend away, clothing, etc. When you live a life full of almost unlimited choices, the world is your oyster, raising the stakes for luxury brands to not only be the best choice in their industry, but likely the best choices amongst *all* the choices their client might have in life at that time.

◆ IN THE END...

IN THE LUXURY MARKET, THE challenge of unlimited choices is also its greatest opportunity. Ultimately, luxury buyers want to feel that their money is well spent. Whether it's a cherished memory, a symbol of success, or a gift that carries meaning, the experience should feel like more a transformation than transaction. By understanding the emotional needs of your clientele, getting them to think differently about your offer, and delivering a promise that feels life-enhancing, you can rise above the noise.

In a world of too many choices, make your offering one that not only earns attention but captures hearts, and you'll find yourself chosen, time and time again. This means going beyond marketing strategies and focusing on delivering an exceptional experience and an emotional connection. It's about demonstrating why your brand deserves to be noticed and remembered in a world full of choices.

WHAT ARE YOU REALLY SELLING?

WHAT IF THE TRUE VALUE of what you're selling isn't the product or service itself, but something intangible and far more meaningful? Many businesses miss this crucial insight, focusing too much on the tangible features of their offerings rather than the emotional and experiential benefits that truly resonate with luxury buyers.

By understanding and selling the intangible—those emotions, experiences, and transformations that customers crave—you can create stronger connections, justify higher prices, and stand out in a crowded market.

FEATURES VS. BENEFITS

WE'VE ALL HEARD THE ADAGE, "Sell benefits, not features." But even seasoned marketers sometimes fall into the trap of focusing on what their product or service *is* rather than what it *does* for the customer.

Features such as the quality of materials, craftsmanship, or the specifications of a service are undoubtedly important and often the central focus of luxury. But features alone rarely inspire a purchase. Customers want to know how those features translate into meaningful benefits for their lives.

In the luxury market, this principle goes even further. It's not just about benefits, it's about the emotional meaning behind the purchase. Luxury buyers, in particular, aren't just buying an item, they're investing in a feeling, an identity, or a moment.

SELLING MORE THAN THE PRODUCT

CONSIDER MY EXPERIENCE AS A luxury portrait photographer. While it may seem that I was selling photographs, I understood that the real value I offered was far more significant.

In conversations with clients, I wouldn't focus solely on the benefits of having portraits as memories or to hand down or even the quality of the finished product. Instead, I would ask them to imagine walking past a portrait of their children or family, prominently displayed on their wall, years into the future. I'd prompt them to envision the size and impact of a portrait that would "stop them in their tracks."

That phrase—"stop them in their tracks" shifted the conversation from being about a product to being about a moment, an emotional experience tied to the memories and meaning encapsulated in the portrait.

SELLING A TRANSFORMATION

IN NON-TANGIBLE BUSINESSES, LIKE COACHING for example, the product isn't the program or the number of calls included. What you're really selling is the transformation your client will experience—the person they can become through your coaching.

For example, you're not selling a fitness program; you're selling confidence, health, and a new sense of vitality. You're not selling marketing services; you're selling growth, freedom, and the ability to focus on what your client does best.

Luxury brands have long mastered this art. They're not just selling a parfum—they're selling emotions and a story about how the parfum transforms your evening, the allure, and may even transform your love life. Imagine that. All that from a fragrance.

JUSTIFYING THE PRICE

IN THE LUXURY MARKET, INTANGIBLE benefits are often what justify the expense. Buyers need to feel that they're investing in more than just a product or service. They're investing in their emotions, aspirations, and identity.

A luxury car or a yacht isn't just a mode of transportation. It's a symbol of success, an invitation to adventure, and a promise of comfort and refinement. The car or yacht's features are important, but they're secondary to the emotional pull of what owning that car represents.

Psychologists have shown that most purchasing decisions are driven by emotion, not logic. Even when customers rationalize their choices afterward, it's their emotional response that tips the scales. By tapping into these emotions, you create a powerful connection that goes beyond the transactional. You're not just selling something, you're becoming part of their story.

AN EXERCISE IN SPEAKING BENEFITS AND TRANSFORMATION

MAKE A LIST OF THE emotions or experiences that your product or service delivers. Consider what you might be inclined to say or have said in the past and ask yourself, "Is this a benefit or a feature?" You might catch yourself speaking features more often than ideal. Of course, if you have a staff, everyone should do this exercise. Use this scripting to refine marketing and sales language to focus on the intangible benefits that matter most to your clientele.

For example, let's consider a jeweler. Rather than solely emphasizing the craftsmanship, focus on how the piece becomes a part of memorable moments and is worn on special occasions or passed down as a cherished family heirloom.

How about travel? Don't just promote the destination; sell the complete emotional experience whether it's the joy of discovering a new culture, the serenity of disconnecting from daily life, or the thrill of adventure.

Perhaps you're an interior designer. In marketing and sales, in addition to the specifics of the design, focus on the most special moments yet to be experienced in the newly designed home.

These are just a few examples in a short sample of industries but I'm confident you can adapt to your own. Imagine how your offering integrates into your customer's life. What role does it play? What moments does it enhance?

To master the art of selling the intangible, you may need to shift your own mindset as well. Instead of seeing yourself as a seller of products or purveyor of services, see yourself as a creator of experiences and emotions.

Your goal isn't just to make a sale—it's to enrich your customer's life in a meaningful way.

◆ IN THE END...

SINCE FEATURES AND QUALITY ARE often assumed, the real differentiator is the intangible. By focusing on the emotions, experiences, and transformations that your product or service delivers, you can create a deeper connection with your audience and stand out in any market. The key is to go beyond what your product *is* and speak to what it *means*. Ask yourself, "What is the intangible promise I'm delivering?"

When you can answer that question and communicate it effectively, you're no longer just selling a product or service. You're creating a story, a moment, a reason to purchase. And that's what customers will remember.

ABASK
Creating an Online Luxury Experience

LUXURY CONSUMERS HAVE TRADITIONALLY PREFERRED in-store shopping to immerse themselves in the sensory and environmental aspects most often associated with luxury. However, one online company, Abask, has successfully brought this market online through a seamless, user-friendly platform.

Abask, founded in 2022 by Tom Chapman and Nicolas Pickaerts, has redefined the online luxury shopping experience by offering a highly curated selection of artisan-crafted homeware and gifts. Abask highlights items of exceptional craftsmanship, design, and quality from makers around the world.

With detailed product descriptions, high-quality imagery, a mission to preserve endangered craftsmanship techniques, and a commitment to a user-friendly platform, they have accomplished the nearly impossible—creating an online luxury experience for the high-end consumer.

What further distinguishes Abask is its attentive, personalized customer service available to support its affluent clientele. They have simplified the process of discovering and acquiring unique, handcrafted goods while ensuring every online shopping experience reflects the care and quality of its offerings.

By focusing on offering a carefully curated selection with a deep understanding of luxury buyers' needs and creating an easy-to-use, frictionless, online experience, Abask enriches the lives of its customers and establishes itself as a premier online destination for sophisticated home design. They stand as a shining example that luxury is possible online.

THE MEANINGFUL ROLE OF LUXURY BRAND SALES ASSOCIATES

LUXURY RETAIL REPRESENTS A PINNACLE of customer experience, where the goal is not merely to sell products but to create memorable interactions. The role of a sales associate is integral to shaping the client's perception of the brand, building trust and relationships, and fostering loyalty.

As a frequent speaker to and shopper within luxury brands, I offer some core principles and best practices for sales associates to consider, from the shopper's perspective.

PRODUCT KNOWLEDGE

MASTERING PRODUCT KNOWLEDGE IS FUNDAMENTAL for every luxury sales associate. Clients expect you to be an expert, capable of offering detailed insights into the products they are interested in. It's not enough to know prices or basic specifications. True expertise lies in understanding the craftsmanship, all options available, and design inspirations that define each piece. Also, a deep appreciation for the brand's heritage and the stories behind iconic designs or collaborations allows you to enrich client interactions with meaningful narratives.

While technology can assist in accessing information, it should never replace genuine expertise. Clients notice when sales associates rely too heavily on websites or their phones to answer simple questions— questions that, quite frankly, the customer could have answered on their own. Instead, technology should serve as a discreet support tool, used only when necessary.

But expertise doesn't stop at products. Sales associates should also have a solid understanding of the broader trends—what makes this choice stand out—and assure the customer they are making a great decision. This helps associates not only sell products but also positions them as experts, reinforcing the brand's value proposition.

PERSONALIZED CUSTOMER SERVICE

Personalization remains the cornerstone of luxury service. Every client interaction should feel unique and tailored to their preferences. By leveraging integrated systems and tools, sales associates can keep track of clients' past purchases and preferences. These tools, when used thoughtfully, enable sales associates to anticipate client needs and provide thoughtful recommendations.

However, personalization isn't just about technology or purchase history. It's about being fully present in the interaction. Take note of small details—a client's preferred style, the importance or usage of the product, or the way they react to certain items. This attentiveness allows associates to craft a more meaningful and memorable experience.

Beyond technology, building strong personal connections is vital. A handwritten thank-you note, a follow-up message, or notifications of new product launches can create meaningful touch points that build loyalty over time. Ultimately, personalization is about making clients feel seen, valued, and understood.

ATTENTION TO DETAIL

In luxury retail, attention to detail extends far beyond product knowledge and experience. Touches such as a glass of champagne or espresso are appreciated and certainly part of the experience. Customers also expect every detail to be perfect, from display and packaging to cleanliness. But these details are expected and therefore not overly impressive.

For a sales associate to make an exceptional impression, in addition to paying attention to the details they provide, take note of details about the customer. For example, when I once stopped in a Dior store to check out a specific pair of sunglasses, the sales associate noticed I was wearing a Dior necklace with the same distinctive logo as the glasses I was interested in, which was my entire motivation in wanting the sunglasses. This level of meticulous attention to detail, not just in presentation but about the customer, makes a meaningful impression. It makes them feel seen and helps reinforce the brand's aspiration for perfection, luxury, and trust. Don't be afraid to make observations and compliment a client's style, preferred color choices, or whatever appears to be significant.

Equally important is the subtlety with which these observations are made. Pointing out details should feel organic, not forced or overly rehearsed. Clients can tell when interactions are contrived or scripted, and nothing breaks the illusion of luxury faster than insincerity.

BALANCING ATTENTIVENESS AND SPACE

BALANCING ATTENTIVENESS WITH RESPECT FOR client autonomy is one of the most nuanced aspects of luxury sales. While clients appreciate attentive service, they also value their space. A skilled associate knows how to read the room, interpreting body language and subtle cues to determine whether a client wants active engagement or time to browse independently. Hovering too closely can feel intrusive, while being too distant may make the client feel neglected.

The ability to step in at the right moment—whether to offer product insights, answer a question, or simply make a suggestion—is a hallmark

of exceptional service. Luxury purchases often require reflection, and clients need space to process their decisions without feeling pressured.

One way to master this balance is to create opportunities for the client to re-engage on their terms. For example, after presenting a product, step back and give them a moment to reflect. A simple, non-intrusive question like, "Would you like me to show you how this pairs with another item?" can open the door without being pushy.

Or if a client is browsing handbags, a sales associate might casually offer a brief insight about one of the designs. "This particular bag was inspired by the architecture of a famous Parisian landmark, and the stitching pattern mirrors its intricate detailing." This approach invites engagement without demanding it. The client is free to continue browsing or use the insight as a conversation starter. It's a subtle but effective way to add value without being intrusive.

PROACTIVE SERVICE

LUXURY BUYERS OFTEN APPRECIATE THOUGHTFUL suggestions, not just because they add value, but because they demonstrate an understanding of their unspoken desires. Proactive service in a luxury context isn't about upselling; it's about creating a sense of being cared for. This level of service begins with attentive listening, not just to what the client says but also to the nuances of their preferences, their past choices, and even the questions they don't ask.

However, the magic of proactive service lies not just in anticipation but in how suggestions are delivered. Tailored recommendations should feel natural, never pushy, and always aligned with the client's personality and values. This subtle difference transforms a transactional suggestion into a personal gesture. When done well, proactive service doesn't just meet expectations—it exceeds them in ways that feel effortless and genuine.

Proactive service also extends to post-purchase care. Following up to ensure satisfaction, offering care tips for a product, or sending a thoughtful message on a special occasion are all ways to continue building trust and connection.

AVOIDING ASSUMPTIONS AND SNOBBERY

IN LUXURY RETAIL, IT IS critical to approach every client with respect and openness, regardless of their appearance or demeanor. Making assumptions about a client's purchasing power or motivations can result in missed opportunities and even damage the brand's reputation. Every client should be treated with the same level of attentiveness and care.

Furthermore, it's essential to remember that luxury purchases often carry emotional significance. Whether commemorating a milestone, celebrating a loved one, or simply indulging in self-care, each purchase has a story. Sales associates who approach these interactions with sensitivity and respect build genuine connections that transcend the transaction.

REPRESENTING THE BRAND

LUXURY SALES ASSOCIATES ARE BRAND ambassadors, embodying the values and ethos of the brand they represent. Every word spoken, every gesture made, and every recommendation contributes to the client's perception of the brand. Confidence, professionalism, and warmth are essential qualities that create trust and foster long-term relationships.

This also means staying composed in challenging situations, whether dealing with a dissatisfied client or navigating a high-pressure moment. Active listening, empathy, and prompt problem-solving demonstrate a commitment to excellence and leave clients with a positive impression, even in less-than-ideal circumstances.

◆ IN THE END...

ULTIMATELY, THE ROLE OF A luxury sales associate extends far beyond transactions. It is about curating experiences, building relationships, and upholding the values of the brand with every interaction and if that is you, a sales associate, you have my utmost respect. Through expertise, personalization, attention to detail, respect for autonomy, and an unwavering commitment to professionalism, sales associates become trusted guides in their clients' luxury journeys. By mastering these principles, you will not only meet but exceed expectations, creating enduring impressions and fostering loyalty that defines true luxury service.

HELPING LUXURY BUYERS JUSTIFY THEIR INVESTMENT

ESTEEMED PERSONAL CARE AND COSMETIC company, L'Oréal, had it right all along with their iconic tagline, "Because you're worth it." That catchy line from 1971 helped women from that era and for many decades after justify not only the purchase but also their right to indulge in caring for themselves. It encouraged women to stand their ground and put themselves first. A simple but brilliant tagline!

A strong emotional driver for luxury buyers is the feeling they deserve the indulgence. Whether it's a break from their demanding lives at a luxurious spa, a special piece of jewelry to commemorate an occasion, recognition of their everyday activities, or a symbol of success, helping the luxury buyer feel they deserve it is a powerful purchasing driver.

LONG-TERM THINKING

BEING IN THE FIELD OF luxury buyer behavior, I'm perhaps more impressed than most when I personally experience a sales associate who does an exceptional job of encouraging me to make a purchase.

One such occasion was when I was purchasing a luxury brand watch. I had a few brands in mind and went to a fine jeweler to consider each style and brand. Of course, the watch I fell in love with was beyond the budget I set for myself. I wanted something special that could be worn for a special occasion but also appropriate for everyday wear.

The sales associate saw me wavering and was quick to step up and ask if I had children, perhaps a son. "Yes, I do," I said. He wisely responded,

"You know, a piece this special is a wonderful item to hand down to your son or perhaps to give to him on a special occasion. It will mean so much coming from his dad." Say no more. Sold.

Luxury buyers tend to be long-term thinkers. They have the financial means to plan and are always thinking about the future, whether it's investments or college education for their children. It was this long-term thinking that was the primary emotional driver for me as a family portrait photographer, expressing the importance of having portraits to hand down from generation to generation and the responsibility parents held to commemorate their children's childhood.

Pointing out the long-term benefits of a purchase to luxury buyers can be exactly what they need to hear to feel good about the investment in luxury goods and services.

BENEFITS OF LONGEVITY

ONE OF THE MOST COMPELLING justifications for investing in luxury goods is the superior quality and craftsmanship. Unlike mass-produced items, luxury products include meticulous attention to detail and the use of premium materials. Luxury items are typically designed to stand the test of time.

However, in a time when wellness, self-care, and mental health have gained tremendous awareness, luxury services also have the advantage of pointing out the benefits of longevity. They are not just serving themselves well today, but the real benefit is how they will feel and look in the future. A terrific leverage point for skin care products and the long-term health benefits of many luxury services.

Also, the benefits of longevity need not end with the buyer! As consumers become more aware of sustainability practices, younger buyers, in particular, like to invest in goods that last longer and create less waste.

INVESTMENT COMPARISON

WHEN MONEY ISN'T AN ISSUE, the world is your oyster. When considering a luxury purchase, be it jewelry, clothing, or something tangible, or an experience such as a vacation or a unique dining experience, luxury buyers will often compare apples to oranges because price is not the main criteria.

Their decision process may not be this bracelet or that necklace or earrings from this brand or that brand. It very well could be this gorgeous piece of jewelry or a long weekend in the Maldives.

A wise sales associate or service provider simply helps the buyer make this comparison. It's not to be ignored but instead offer the pros and cons of the decision they are trying to make, even if it's not clear what the comparison is. Help the buyer feel all the reasons that making this purchase is the right emotional decision, that when compared to almost anything else, they will be glad they did.

◆ IN THE END...

LUXURY BUYERS DON'T BASE THEIR decisions solely on price but are influenced by powerful emotional triggers. Helping them justify their investment involves addressing these emotional drivers. They need to feel they deserve the purchase, whether it's an indulgence or a symbol of success. Highlighting long-term benefits, such as value or longevity, appeals to their future-focused mindset. Guiding them to make decisions by comparing the emotional value of one choice against another can help them see why a purchase feels right. By understanding and leveraging these emotions, luxury providers can guide buyers toward decisions they feel genuinely good about.

SIMON PEARCE
Experiential Sales

SIMON PEARCE, KNOWN FOR ITS exceptional glassware and pottery, excels in craftsmanship, authenticity, and relationship-building by creating immersive experiences. What sets the brand apart is how it uses its *experience-based retail* strategy to forge deeper connections with customers.

At its flagship store and workshop in Quechee, Vermont—itself a huge tourist destination—customers can witness artisans handcrafting glassware in real-time, using centuries-old techniques. This behind-the-scenes access transforms a simple shopping trip into an educational and emotional experience. Visitors gain a profound appreciation for the artistry, labor, and care that goes into each piece. It's not just a purchase—it's a memory—a story to take home.

You can then sit down for a fine dining experience with the table, of course, adorned with Simon Pearce products. Having been there many times, believe me, it is impossible to leave without taking home some, if not many, of the exquisite products you have seen made and interacted with. It's sales experience genius. Their entire team is trained not just to sell but to educate and create an experience.

Moreover, Simon Pearce prioritizes personalized service. From hand-written thank-you notes for large purchases to invitations to private events and tours, the brand treats customers as partners in its journey rather than mere consumers.

This combination of experience, education, and thoughtful engagement creates a connection to the brand and the products. Customers don't just buy Simon Pearce products—they are emotionally engaged at every step.

MOMENTS OF HUMANITY

The Hidden Secret of Luxury Sales

IN LUXURY SALES, IT ISN'T as much about what you are selling but rather how you make someone feel. The moment you create in the sales environment does much of the selling. And the most memorable moments for clients—the ones that create lasting connections—aren't the grand gestures or extravagant touches. They are the unassuming moments of humanity.

These are the moments when a service provider or sales associate steps beyond the sales transaction and into the heart of connection. It's a shared laugh, presence and listening, and genuine acknowledgment of the person in front of you. This is the hidden secret of luxury sales—the quiet moments of humanity that elevate the experience and build trust.

Luxury clients are often surrounded by excellence. They expect a lot. What they don't expect, but deeply appreciate, are more intimate moments in sales environments that slow them down, and make them feel understood and fully supported toward their best choices.

When we think of luxury, we often think of tangible products and acts of service. But the real magic of luxury sales lies in the intangibles. It's how a client feels during and after the interaction—valued, seen, and deeply connected to the service provider and the choices they make. At every moment in a sales environment, you have an opportunity to make your clients feel valued not just as purchasers but as people.

When selling luxury, your role is not just to sell—it's to elevate.

Here are some ways you can create those elevated moments:

- **Acknowledging Significance**

    Often a client will share if they are commemorating a special occasion—an anniversary dinner, a birthday massage, or a piece

of jewelry to celebrate a milestone. Of course, these moments must be acknowledged. But not all clients are as forthcoming so it's always worth asking, "Is there significance for you in this purchase?" Offer them an opportunity to be in the moment of celebration. Also, be prepared to support them should the moment be to commemorate a loss. Perhaps the choice of a special necklace to honor the loss of a parent or child. Spa services needed for self-care and recovery. Luxury purchases often celebrate something wonderful and can also be a moment to honor. However, as their service provider, it is always best to be prepared to hold space for whatever the person before you is experiencing. Allowing them space to bring that out is often better than leaving it unsaid. It's not just about the product but about sharing a moment in their life.

- **A Shared Laugh**

  I often find a shared laugh or a little injection of humor and lightness is a great way to ease the decision process when making a significant purchase. Of course, appropriate use of humor is imperative, never directed at anyone, but just the humor of life. I'm always reminded of the Jerry Seinfeld show which was often described as a show about nothing. But Jerry Seinfeld himself described it as a show about anything. There is humor and lightness to be found in any moment. Leveraging those moments to ease the pressure during high-end sales can be very effective. In fact, observe how often a lighter moment will be followed by, "OK, I'll take it." What you're doing with carefully selected moments of humor is shifting the mood and removing decision fog, so your customer can make a clear decision.

- **Slow It Down**

  Luxury should never be rushed, especially a significant purchase. Of course, if they are truly in a hurry, rushing in to make a last-minute purchase before a birthday celebration, the best sales service you can provide is to be efficient. But often, slowing them down is greatly appreciated. Invite conversation and give them time to review their options without any expression of frustration. If a customer is struggling to make a decision, ask what's going on for them. Invite them to talk it out and give sincere guidance in return, always focused on their best interest and not a bigger sale. Carefully presented, often suggesting the lesser choice will activate all the reasons why they know in their heart it's the larger purchase they want. But if you suggest the larger purchase it could come across as pushy. These are the moments that have the potential to put the luxurious in luxury. Unhurried, fully present, conscious decision-making moments.

- **Remembering Details**

  Very important for repeat customers, remember the moment you shared in the past. If the purchase was a gift, ask how the recipient felt about the gift. If it's a repeat service, remember their preference or details about their family, home, or why they engaged in the service in the past. I've had many meaningful moments when a sales associate remembers a previous exchange where I assumed I was just another customer to them. It's inspiring to imagine being so kind, considerate, and capable of remembering people and details so well, and something we should all aspire to do.

- **Be Fully Present**

  In luxury sales, always be fully present. Avoid multitasking or being distracted and give the client your undivided attention. These uninterrupted moments when they occur in life feel rare and special. You are the curator of a moment and a tour guide on their

way to making an important choice. It requires artfully knowing when to be still and when to step in. You can only do this at an exceptional level if you are fully present in the moment. Whether it's a large or small luxury purchase, there is likely significance to the moment for the customer.

◆ IN THE END...

DONE WITH LESS INTENTION, LUXURY sales can feel transactional, but the most meaningful and memorable interactions are deeply human. As a luxury business owner or sales associate, you have the power to create moments that matter—not through grand gestures but through simple, authentic moments of humanity.

Remember, luxury isn't just about the product or service. It's about the experience and the connection. At the heart of that connection are the unassuming moments that bring humanity into the luxury space. These moments are what clients remember, and they are the hidden secret to exceptional sales. It's not about selling—it's about elevating.

YOUR DIAMOND EDGE

You are more capable, more extraordinary,
and more valuable than you may ever
fully realize on your own.

YOUR DIAMOND EDGE

You may have noticed the diamond motif throughout this book. On the cover, in the page design, and my aforementioned LinkedIn newsletter called Diamond Edge. There are layers upon layers of meaning behind the diamond motif for me, and I'll share the most significant reason in a moment. But before I do, let me point out the most important thing about this, which is *your* Diamond Edge.

Icons and symbols have long been an important part of luxury brands, each carrying a story and a significance far beyond the design itself. Like my chosen icon—the diamond—these symbols represent a discovery within oneself that becomes a bold statement to the world. These emblems become timeless beacons that guide the brand through changing markets, fluctuating economies, and shifting cultural tides. Rolex's five-point crown represents "A crown for every achievement." Cartier's panther embodies grace, power, and untamed spirit. The Medusa head of Versace speaks of allure and irresistible beauty. These icons aren't just logos—they are storytellers.

My diamond story dates back to the 1980s when I was rebranding my photography business for the high-end market. What it represented then still holds true today, albeit in an evolution of my brand and line of work.

At first, my portrait photography business had a catchy photography name—Light Images. Clever, right? But one of the most significant discoveries I made while studying luxury brands at that time was that personal brands were very popular and held a cachet. It was the rise of personal branding like Ralph Lauren and Martha Stewart. It was then that I decided that to capture the attention of an affluent clientele and assure them they were getting something special, unique, and personal, my business name should be simply Jeffrey Shaw.

The difference though, between myself and other iconic personal brands, was that while I intended to grow, I didn't intend to scale at large. I worked with a graphic artist to design my logo, business card, and packaging, and he, however, seemed to have a different idea. He kept insisting I call my business Jeffrey Shaw Photographers or Jeffrey Shaw and Associates, so certain that my business would grow and I would want to hire additional photographers. I had a very different business model in mind. It was my intention that as my business grew, I would raise rates to control volume which would consistently push up profitability. I would remain as the only photographer and hire a team for everything else. Office staff, photography assistants, retouchers, framers, and even support at home, all to free me up to do the only two tasks I needed to focus on: photography and selling.

As he continued to insist that I have a "scalable name," I grew more and more frustrated with his lack of listening. At some point I stated quite boldly, "It's Jeffrey Shaw. Period."

The following week he presented me with the next iteration of my logo. With a certain amount of indignance and maybe intended humor, he showed me a logo of my name with a period at the end, just after my name. I looked at it carefully. I paused. I'm pretty sure I leaned my head to one side and then the other as if viewing it from different angles. When done with my very careful consideration, I looked at him and said, "Change the period to a diamond and we're all set."

He was shocked. Maybe he thought it was ridiculous. But I didn't give him a chance to respond and frankly, I didn't care. I was already walking out the door of his office, knowing in my bones that this was right for me. That diamond wasn't going to be just a design element, it was a declaration. A representation of my confidence, my self-worth, my clarity of vision, my unwavering belief in my path, and my business model. It symbolized my personal growth, the challenges I'd overcome, the honesty and integrity I stood for, and the extraordinary value I was committed to delivering. I sensed that to succeed with this clientele I would have to present a business that was clear, straightforward, had no gimmicks or unnecessary fanfare, with a passion to serve, and always with clean energy, confident in who I was. It was always going to be Jeffrey Shaw. Period. He had been working so hard to take away from me what I had worked so hard to claim. My diamond edge. The clarity and sharpness that came from a willingness to grow and challenge myself. It wouldn't be the last time I'd face a naysayer, have my path challenged, or face my own doubts.

I simply changed his idea (based on my declaration) from a period to a diamond because even at twenty-three years old, I had the wherewithal to know a diamond connotated affluence.

What I couldn't know at that time is that many years later, a Buddhist writing called The Diamond Sutra would have a profound effect on my business philosophies when I learned how our every action has a reciprocal effect. What we put out, we get in return. While the essence of the teaching may seem like karma, it's actually a bit different. It's more about correlations; understanding how our thoughts and behavior may correlate to a result we're seeing but not be directly related. For example, the mindset gap I spoke of in Element II. There's nothing wrong with shopping at The Dollar Store per se, but being in the constant pursuit of discounts can correlate to your inability to get others to see your value. With this understanding, I started taking responsibility for everything I saw and all the results I received. I believe this is when the deepest levels of empathy and a desire to understand behavior really opened up for me.

This eternal lesson is called The Diamond Sutra because a diamond can only be cut by another diamond. It teaches us that only we can cut through our own blocks and limitations to discover the diamond within ourselves. Our greatness. As we allow the greatness within us to be pulled out by those we surround ourselves with and those we step up to serve, we discover our Diamond Edge—our sharpness and our clarity—which becomes our advantage because we have done the work to be exceptional.

This is the opportunity that lies within serving the luxury market. You are choosing to work with a clientele that is sophisticated, has high standards—may at times feel demanding because they are always calling forward the best from you—and remains very perceptive to good and bad intentions. In doing so, you are stepping into your greatness.

Because here's the truth. You are more capable, more extraordinary, and more valuable than you may ever fully realize on your own. The world you're stepping into isn't reserved for others—it's waiting for *you*. Your vision matters. Your voice matters. Your unique brilliance is not something to be hidden or softened, it's something to be sharpened, celebrated, and shared. If I opened the opportunity for myself from where I started, so can you. Whether you are a business owner offering a luxury service or product, a sales associate on the front line of a luxury brand, or leading a team at an established luxury brand, doing business with the luxury buyer is an open invitation for growth in all its forms.

Confidence isn't a luxury, it's inherent. Self-worth isn't conditional, it's your birthright. The journey ahead of you may not always be easy, but the richness you'll discover—in your clients, your work, and most importantly, in yourself—will make every step worth it.

Let me say this simply. You can do this. You are worthy of this. You deserve this.

If you've doubted yourself, let this moment mark the end of that doubt. If you've played small, let this be the moment you step fully into your boldness. And if you've ever wondered whether you belong in this space, let me remind you—you do.

Now move forward with clarity and courage and with the unshakable knowledge that your Diamond Edge isn't just a symbol—it's the connecting element between you and those waiting for you to show up.

And this my friend, is how you sell to the rich.

ACKNOWLEDGMENTS

"A rising tide lifts all boats."
—President John F. Kennedy

IF THERE'S ONE NOTION I have embraced over the years—and will continue to focus on in the years ahead—it is the spirit of collaboration. An energy that's different than hiring people, different than teamwork, and different than masterminding. Collaboration brings together, in partnership or as a group, the talent and character of each individual. In a word, their greatness. In this environment, truly a rising tide lifts all boats. I am better because of the following collaborators.

Kristina Paider, my editor extraordinaire, wow, thank you. Your patience was exceptional, your ideas brilliant, your attention to detail extreme, and well, you're also a blast to play with! Thank you for never letting up on helping to bring out the character and heart of the book.

Paul Cuneo, my sherpa along this Hero's Journey, in many ways you brought this entire idea to light. You helped me find my road back to where I belong. And then you helped with some of the copywriting to be sure I stayed true to my path and the heart of the book stayed intact. Thank you, my friend.

Sharon Hobson, thank you for "getting me" and creating a cover design that has meaning, stays on brand, and supports my entire body of work. No small feat.

Choi Messer, as we discussed, the environment of this book was essential to supporting the content. The layout and pages you created are masterful and meaningful. You are an incredible talent and I thank you.

Anna Paradox, details are an important component of luxury. Not because we strive for perfection, but for the benefit and experience of the user. I knew you got me from the moment we met, and you really did. Thank you for your meticulous care in copyediting, deepening what was meaningful and simplifying what was complicated.

AJ Harper, my always present sounding board and advisor. Thank you for your generosity, support, and mostly for being you. One should be so lucky to have an AJ in their life.

The collaboration and support I receive goes beyond the book.

Thank you to my beautiful daughter, Clare, who is my business support, life support, and so very wise council. I couldn't do this work and life thing without you.

To Rob, my love and life partner, I knew the moment we met that my soul had been waiting for you when I said on our first date, "Where the hell have you been?" I love you.

To the members of my High Achievers groups, you are all the best of the best. By that I mean not only the best at what you do but even more importantly, the best people of character, integrity, and an intention to make a difference in the world. You all amaze me.

If we can be blessed with even just a few friends in this life that love you unconditionally and are always there for you, that is a life fulfilled. Nancy and Roger Pelissier and Mary Rooney are the friends most people could only dream about. Love you all.

To my son, Connor, daughter Lilly, and ex-wife, Arlene, none of this would have been possible over the years without your love, support, and more than anything, the inspiration to be more and do better.

THE SELL TO THE RICH KEYNOTE

IF YOUR EVENT CATERS TO professionals who sell to high-end clients, International speaker Jeffrey Shaw's *Sell to the Rich* keynote is the show-stopping session you're looking for.

Luxury buyers think differently, act differently, and buy differently. Understanding their complex behavior and nuanced mindset isn't just a skill—it's an art. Jeffrey brings decades of real-world experience and insider knowledge, delivering an unforgettable keynote that takes your audience behind the curtain to reveal exactly what makes the affluent tick.

From emotional triggers to behavior patterns, Jeffrey shares actionable strategies that redefine how attendees approach the luxury market. Forget generic sales tactics—this talk dives deep into the psychographics, lifestyle, and expectations of the affluent, showing your audience how to not only sell but build lasting brand loyalty with this uncompromising clientele.

Whether it's attracting ideal luxury clients, overcoming objections, creating brand obsession, or adapting to the ever-changing landscape, Jeffrey's talk is packed with insights attendees can implement immediately.

With a deep understanding of affluent clients and a dynamic, engaging style, Jeffrey ensures your audience will leave inspired, enlightened, and equipped with tools to elevate their success in the luxury space.

Book Jeffrey for your next event and give your audience a keynote experience they'll thank you for—one that transforms how they sell to the rich.

Find out more at
www.jeffreyshawspeaks.com